Dirty Little Secrets
Real-Life Stories from the Midlands

Copyright © 2014 Good Catch Publishing, Beaverton, OR.

All rights reserved. Written permission must be secured from the publisher to use or reproduce any part of this book, except for brief quotations in critical reviews or articles.

This book was written for the express purpose of conveying the love and mercy of Jesus Christ. The statements in this book are substantially true; however, names and minor details have been changed to protect people and situations from accusation or incrimination.

All Scripture quotations, unless otherwise noted, are taken from the New International Version Copyright 1973, 1984, 1987 by International Bible Society.

Published in Beaverton, Oregon, by Good Catch Publishing.
www.goodcatchpublishing.com
V1.1

Printed in the United States of America

Table of Contents

	Acknowledgements	9
	Introduction	13
1	Lone Wolf Adoption	15
2	Beauty for Ashes	43
3	He Was Always There	71
4	Free From Me	89
5	Living With a Purpose	121
6	Alive Again	143
7	The Answer	171
	Conclusion	205

Acknowledgements

I would like to thank Randy Knechtel and Chuck Hill for their vision for this book and for their hard work in making it a reality. And to the people of Vive, thank you for your boldness and vulnerability in sharing your personal stories.

This book would not have been published without the amazing efforts of our project manager and editor, Debbie Allen. Her untiring resolve pushed this project forward and turned it into a stunning victory. Thank you for your great fortitude and diligence. Deep thanks to our incredible editor in chief, Michelle Cuthrell, and executive editor, Jen Genovesi, for all the amazing work they do. I would also like to thank our invaluable proofreader, Melody Davis, for the focus and energy she has put into perfecting our words.

Lastly, I want to extend our gratitude to the creative and very talented Jenny Randle, who designed the beautiful cover for *Dirty Little Secrets: Real-Life Stories from the Midlands.*

Daren Lindley
President and CEO
Good Catch Publishing

The book you are about to read
is a compilation of authentic life stories.
The facts are true, and the events are real.
These storytellers have dealt with crisis, tragedy, abuse
and neglect and have shared their most private moments,
mess-ups and hang-ups in order for others to learn and
grow from them. In order to protect the identities of those
involved in their pasts, the names and details of some
storytellers have been withheld or changed.

Introduction

What do you do when life is careening out of control? When addiction has overtaken you or abuse chained you with fear? Is depression escapable? Will relationships ever be healthy again? Are we destined to dissolve into an abyss of sorrow? Or will the sunlight of happiness ever return?

Your life really can change. It is possible to become a new person. The seven stories you are about to read prove positively that people right here in the Midlands have stopped dying and started living. Whether you've been beaten by abuse, broken promises, shattered dreams or suffocating addictions, the resounding answer is, "Yes! You can become a new person." The potential to break free from gloom and into a bright future awaits.

Expect inspiration, hope and transformation! As you walk with real people from our very own community through the pages of this book, you will not only find riveting accounts of their hardships, you will learn the secrets that brought about their breakthroughs. These people are no longer living in the shadows of yesterday; they are thriving with a sense of mission and purpose TODAY. May these stories inspire you to do the same.

Lone Wolf Adoption
The Story of Richard
Written by Douglas Abbott

My earliest clear memory is when I was 4. Mommy and I were home alone that day, and I was watching television in the living room around mid-morning when I noticed that the kitchen sounds — the crinkling of bags, Mommy's knife against the cutting board, cupboards opening and closing — had stopped. I left watching Bugs Bunny and walked around the corner into the kitchen.

Mommy was lying on the floor in front of the sink. Her legs were sprawled strangely in different directions, and one of her arms lay pinned underneath her. I couldn't understand why she was so tired that she would sleep on the kitchen floor in the middle of the day. She didn't look comfortable at all, and she had left the water running. I went back into the living room to finish the Bugs Bunny cartoon.

A while later, I went back to see if Mommy was awake yet, but she was still asleep in the same position while the faucet ran and ran. I began to feel scared.

"Get up, Mommy!" I shook her over and over. But she didn't wake up, no matter how loudly I called, no matter how hard I shook her.

I would never hear her voice again.

By evening of the day my mother died, our house filled up with police, paramedics and weepy family members. My father trudged around with a waxy, disconnected look on his face. After all the commotion died down, my grandparents excused themselves and took me home with them.

I don't remember my mother's funeral or much of anything else for the next several weeks. Of course, I had no concept of death. I was upset at my mother for going away.

My feelings alternated between anger, sadness and warm memory fragments of Mommy playing with me in the yard and dressing me up in tiny plaid suits.

A few months later, my father remarried. Shortly after the wedding, we moved into an apartment on the outskirts of town.

My stepmother, Peggy, hated me, apparently because I was a visual reminder of my father's previous marriage. I was another of her unpleasant chores.

One time, I awakened in the middle of the night to a throbbing pain in my face.

"Daddy, look!" I said, standing in the doorway of his bedroom. "My face is cut." It was my simple way of describing the deep scratches in my left cheek.

My father got up and washed and bandaged my face. "Looks like the cat got to him," Peggy said.

He went along with the assessment, but I heard my grandparents arguing with my father and Peggy about it a few nights later, when they thought I was asleep.

"Those scratches weren't made by a cat," my grandfather said as they sat in the living room. "Those are people scratches. We want to know what's going on here."

Two months later, Peggy gave birth to my half brother, Paul. I was too young to add or to know about the nine-month gestation period. My father's infidelity would be an unpleasant realization for later.

One evening not long after Paul's birth, Peggy laid two large knives at the foot of Paul's bed. When my father arrived home, Peggy told him she had caught me in Paul's room with the knives.

"I found a chair in the kitchen underneath the knife case," Peggy said. "Richard must have used it to reach the knives. Something needs to be done."

The something was what Peggy had wanted all along — to get rid of me. After a few more months of her focused loathing, my mom's parents stepped in. My grandfather was a Chicago police officer, well connected enough to cause trouble for my father if he didn't play along. My father, an auditor for the IRS at the time, had no desire to complicate his life further, particularly with a new wife and an infant son to look after.

"We're going to adopt Richard," my grandparents insisted. So I went to live under their roof. For the next several years, life was considerably less tumultuous. I found myself sharing a house with my mom's younger brothers and sisters, who still lived at home and whom I had previously seen only during holiday gatherings or other special occasions. Life was filled with normal little-boy things — elementary school, *Sesame Street*, Tonka trucks and Erector sets.

I was the Golden Child. For some reason, perhaps the tragedy that had caused me to come live there, I was given preferential treatment. Uncle Philip had to share his room with me. I could do no wrong. When Christmas came around, there were always piles of presents for me under the tree.

By the time I was 10, my aunts and uncles had each come of age and moved out of the house. The atmosphere at home changed.

My grandparents began to drink more and started to be mean to me. I started to lose respect for the house rules. On one occasion, my experimentation with matches provoked my grandfather to tie me to the washer and beat me with a police belt.

Something was happening to their minds. One evening, after my latest display of independence, I lay in bed while my grandparents stood outside my door and discussed which knives they should employ to punish me.

"No, that's not sharp enough," my grandfather was saying.

"Well, the one you've got isn't nearly big enough," Grandmother said.

"We don't want it to be too big," Granddad came back. "It's got to go between the ribs."

Fortunately, I never had to find out whether there was real murderous intent or just alcohol talking that night. Aunt Monica came in time to overhear their discussion, after which she took me home with her while they cooled down.

My grandparents' drunkenness increased, as did their rage. At the height of their impairment, they each drank a case of beer every night. They began to have violent conflicts. The house shook as they overturned furniture and hurled objects through windows. My grandfather began using his fists on Grandmother, but nobody stopped him. I figured it was because he was a police officer. Finally, a series of strokes disabled him, and around the same time, my grandmother suffered an aneurysm that degraded her mental capacity. A crippled quasi-peace settled over the house. By this time, I was 13, doing mostly whatever I wanted and helping myself to my grandparents' things, including their booze. Now, when my grandmother discovered my misdeeds, she growled at me. It was at once safer and more frightening than it had been before. None of my friends ventured into the house anymore.

After my grandfather passed away, Aunt Marcy moved into the basement of the house with her husband, Jared, both to help care for my ailing grandmother and to parent me. By this time, it was clear to the entire family that I had been shortchanged in many ways during my upbringing. Because there had been no cohesive structure in my life, I had invented myself in a haphazard, self-styled fashion. I was 15 years old and had come to enjoy calling my own shots. My adjustment to life's thrashings was to assume a posture of strength and confidence. I was smart, capable and moved to dominate the scene wherever I went. I was going to rule the world.

Hence, Uncle Jared's well-intentioned effort to parent me was a failure. I was a bitter, angry young man, still smarting from the loss of my mother and mistrustful of adults. I had lived for years in self-indulgence with the view that other people were there for my use and pleasure. The sudden imposition of boundaries by my well-meaning uncle-in-law was unacceptable to me. I began rebelling against him and Aunt Marcy with gusto. I smoked pot as often as I could get hold of it, drank alcohol, shoplifted and ignored my curfew.

I didn't think much about it then, but now I think my antisocial behavior was fueled by bitterness toward the God, whatever and whoever he was, who had stolen away the only person I had ever loved. From time to time, gauzy images of my mother's smiling face penetrated my angry consciousness. When they did, I clenched my fists and swore I would pay God back for what he had done to me.

One day, my aunt and uncle announced that we were going to move from the city into the suburbs of Chicago. Grandma had moved in with my other uncle. I was completely opposed to the move. While the house was being repaired in order to put it up for sale, I went around damaging the work to sabotage the move. But in the end, there was little I could do to thwart it. All our worldly goods were soon packed into the back of a U-Haul.

Once ensconced in the suburbs, I quickly set out to establish myself in the way I had grown accustomed. I started a gang called the Morgan Park Motorheads, which dominated the park for which it was named. Meanwhile, I resumed my daily routine of drinking, drugging and larceny.

"You don't know what you're doing to yourself," Uncle Jared told me more than once. "It's easy to burn bridges *now*. The problem is, someday you're going to need them." But I was unmoved.

When I turned 16, Aunt Marcy and Uncle Jared threw in the towel.

"You're on your own," Uncle Jared said. Weariness and exasperation creased his face as he said the words. We were sitting in the living room of their new apartment. Aunt Marcy sat next to him on the couch, and I could see both anger and sadness in her features.

"What, because I won't march to the beat of your crusty little drum?" I said sarcastically.

"You're out of control," Uncle Jared said stonily. "We didn't take you into our home so you could use it for a flophouse. You don't follow any of our rules. You're destructive. And you're a complete ingrate."

"I didn't ask for your charity," I snarled back at him. Before long, the brouhaha moved from the house down the steps and onto the lawn.

"Here, have your crappy watch back," I said, unclasping the gold watch they had given me for my birthday. "I never liked it, anyway." I hurled it at him, but it went through the screen door instead, making a satisfying tinkle and a mess of shattered glass.

Dirty Little Secrets

"Get out of here, NOW!" Uncle Jared bellowed, standing up and advancing toward me. His face and neck were nearly purple.

I turned to leave with a contemptuous swagger, jumped into my car and drove away.

I moved back into the city and lived in my 1967 Ranchero for a month. While I gathered my resources for better lodging, I continued attending school, where I discovered I was a natural on computers. Both to see what I could do and just to be a jerk, I got on a classroom computer, infiltrated the school mainframe, printed up a whole batch of faculty payroll checks and brought them into the office to flaunt my handiwork.

"You're banned from all the computers," Principal Walters growled at me in his office the next day. "You're lucky I don't throw your a** out of here."

I got back into the system, changed the access codes and locked the faculty out of the system. That afternoon, I was once again in Principal Walters' office with three school administrators scowling across from me.

"You realize you can't attend school here anymore," Principal Walters said. It was more of a statement than a question. "So we tallied your credits. You have enough to graduate. If you give us the codes, you can take your diploma and go."

As I strutted out, Principal Walters called after me, "Just in case you were wondering, you're not allowed on these premises anymore."

I knew he wanted to do more to me, but because my

Lone Wolf Adoption

ragamuffin emancipation had left me without any family authority over me, he had no way of imposing any real punishment. Through a hundred situations just like this, I had learned I didn't have to pay for my misconduct. I counted myself too smart, quick and clever to get hit. And for a long while, it seemed to be true.

❧❧❧

I joined the Air Force when I was 17. The idea came to me as I stretched out on a mattress in the unfinished basement of a house belonging to my friend Pete's parents. They had heard I was camping in my Ranchero and invited me to their home. However, after a few months of gazing at floor joists and bare concrete, I knew I couldn't stay. I had plans to make my presence known in the world, but here I was living like a vagabond and drinking like a fish. I felt like I had no future. So I went down to the recruiter's office.

When I submitted a near-perfect ASVAB (Armed Services Vocational Aptitude Battery), the recruiter told me I could literally do anything I wanted in the Air Force. I told him I wanted to be a nuclear weapons specialist. The fact that I would end up working with nuclear weapons (the most powerful device in the world) meshed well with my grandiose ideas.

Within a few weeks, I arrived at Lackland Air Force Base in San Antonio, Texas, for boot camp.

The rigorous training might have challenged me

mentally and physically if it hadn't been for my artistic ability.

I noticed my drill instructor assembling a podium out of oak wood. When he commented that he was less than satisfied with the finished product, I drew up some designs and showed them to him.

"I can paint this pattern on the front of the podium and spice it right up, sir," I told him.

The sergeant studied the sheet of paper for a moment, then looked up at me with a delighted grin. "You can make the front of my lectern look like this?" he asked.

"Oh, yes, sir!"

All of a sudden, I was dodging all the worst parts of Basic Training — KP, GI parties, long runs and anything else I didn't feel like doing. It was the kind of thing that always happened — my talent and shrewdness permitted me to get around the requirements. It had been happening to me for so long, I thought it was my birthright.

After Basic Training, I went to Lowry Air Force Base in Denver. Advanced training was well within my grasp, and I seldom broke a sweat. I made great money and stayed in plush quarters. It was too easy to forget why I had joined the military in the first place, especially with an NCO club right across from the barracks.

There was no age limit for drinking on the base, so at the tender age of 17, I was soon drinking profusely, supplied with large weekly checks, a high-limit charge card at the club and a great affinity for the grog. Soon, I was doing nothing but attending school and drinking.

Lone Wolf Adoption

It was a continuation of the same story: Because I was intelligent and high-functioning, I could go around like a slobbering drunk and still score in the top 10 percent in my classes. Between classes, I would visit the vending machines in the hall, where I employed a new trick I had learned to get free sandwiches. Somehow, I figured out how to keep the lazy Susan turning after the door was already open. I would pay for a single sandwich, open the door, then grab another 10 sandwiches for free as they marched by on the track. I even taught the trick to my buddies.

಄಄಄

I was stationed at Whiteman Air Force Base in Missouri. It was my first permanent base assignment. I received another raise in pay, bought a brand-new motorcycle and settled into the nightlife there. It was my misfortune that the base housing was directly across from the NCO club, where I lived whenever I wasn't on duty or in classes. At the club, I met my first wife, Stephanie, a winsome, lovely girl impressed with my hot wheels and my Air Force career. We married within a few months.

Stephanie's father was my first sergeant. When we got married, Sergeant Lowell pulled me aside for a talk.

"Son, there's no question you're bright and capable. Why do you insist on doing things that get you in trouble?"

I leveled with him. "I've got a drinking problem, sir."

"Oh, it's not that bad."

"If you don't believe me, check my bill at the NCO club."

So he did, and they told him my bill for the month (with a week remaining) was $1,700, which in today's dollars would be around $4,500.

Sergeant Lowell came to see me in the barracks the next day. "You're going to Shepard Air Force Base," he told me.

"Oh, wow. That sounds cool."

"You're not transferring. You're going there for rehab. You'll be there for 45 days. You will attend AA meetings, sober up, and when you come back here, we're going to go on with our lives."

The idea of doing rehab was onerous to me. However, I found a silver lining. Over the prior year, I had grown bored with my job, but whenever I asked to cross-train, I was turned down. Now that I was headed to Shepard, I learned that no known alcoholic was allowed to work with nuclear weapons. This was my ticket out of being bored to tears for the next 20 years.

I had outsmarted everyone, again.

I arrived in Southern Texas and discovered that Shepard was a mental institution.

How in the world did I end up here? I thought. No matter. I approached my stint in rehab as I had approached everything else in my life: I mastered the system. I learned the rules, the politics and the people. While the staff there learned nothing about me, I learned everything about them and how they went about treating Air Force drunks. I exhibited all the caring, sincere sentiments they were looking for, spoke the recovery language and even became the patient foreman before I had been there two weeks. Nothing changed. King Richard had done the usual and taken charge. I flew through the program in spite of going AWOL one night to have both forearms tattooed off base.

Back at Whiteman, I was told I had two choices: be a cook or go into MWR (Morale, Welfare and Recreation). I chose MWR, which had me helping run gyms, recreation centers, NCO and Ermine clubs. In spite of spending so much time working with alcohol, I stayed sober.

Stephanie and I were far from being in love, but we kept a house together, partly because I was still under the authority of Stephanie's father. Two years crept by, during which I did my job well, looked after my affairs and stayed away from the drink.

"You're going to Avon Park, Florida," my commanding officer informed me after another year had gone by. My adventures at Shepard were all but forgotten. Stephanie's father and mother were being transferred to San Francisco.

So Stephanie and I did the Next Thing in Florida, where I bought my first Harley-Davidson and got a dozen more tattoos. I was what might have been referred to as "Nouveau Air Force," but it worked. I got involved in area biker clubs and kept at my Air Force duties. My superiors didn't have an inkling anything was brewing, and it wasn't, for the moment. I even had lunch with General Norman Schwarzkopf.

I got the note when I least expected it:

Richard,

    I'm sorry. I can't do this anymore. Being separated from my family is killing me. I'm going to San Francisco. I wish you the best.

Stephanie

I filed for divorce without shedding a tear. I had long felt that Stephanie and I were doing little more than playing house.

It didn't escape me that I was now a highly paid single man with an enviable career, a dream lifestyle and a Harley-Davidson to boot.

I took a side job as a bouncer and blackjack dealer. It didn't occur to me to be concerned about working in a bar. As far as I knew, staying sober was as easy as everything else in life. I could do it in my sleep. But I didn't. That was the year I both resumed my love affair with booze and married my second wife, Shari.

My firstborn son, Robert, came into the world in June of 1988, followed closely by Aliea in 1990. Things were deceptively stable. The Air Force had proved to be an easy career — so easy that having a family and working side jobs was quite manageable.

The first sign of trouble came one afternoon when I

arrived home and found a mirror in the bathroom with streaks of white powder on it.

"What's this?" I asked Shari, setting the mirror down on the coffee table in the living room.

"I tried meth," she said, the same way she might have said, "I got a speeding ticket." Somehow, I wasn't concerned. Up until now, I didn't have any experience with "hard" drugs. It was 1990, after all, and most of the country, including us, had no idea how dangerous methamphetamine was. Shari told me she had used the stimulant effect to help her clean the entire house.

Meanwhile, I decided to re-enlist in the Air Force. I was creeping up on the 10-year mark, and the thought of going for 20 years was attractive, particularly considering that I could then retire with partial pay and benefits.

My comfortable middle-class world began to fracture not long after I signed for another term. While I was away at work, money began to come up missing. The house took on a punched, neglected look. It was constantly cluttered and dirty. Finally, I discovered that Shari had begun collecting welfare checks. She had gone to the state and told them I abandoned her.

Next, Shari began turning up with a boyfriend — a meth dealer, no less. While I contemplated how to deal with this, I was called into a meeting with my Air Force commander, Sergeant Major Briggs.

"Mr. Fallon, your services are no longer needed," the sergeant major said crisply. "You will be leaving the Air Force."

I had heard about the reduction in defense spending, but I hadn't seen this coming.

"We will give you $22,000 to help you get on with your life," he added.

That was something I could get behind. Without giving it much thought, I signed the paperwork, collected my things from the base and returned home. I was a civilian again.

I bought a new Harley-Davidson to soothe myself. Somehow, I couldn't bear to look directly at the way my life was unraveling. That would be a reckoning for later. In the meantime, I got a job working as a whitewater rafting guide in Silva, North Carolina. It was a fantastic job, but I was soon joining the other guides in drinking profusely and smoking pot regularly. Before long, I broke down and tried meth with Shari. In a strange, toxic way, it brought togetherness back into my marriage for a time. I discovered how productive I could be when fatigue was taken out of the picture.

The attractions in Silva staled quickly, so I moved the family back to Florida while I went to school to become a Harley-Davidson mechanic. I had always loved Harleys, so it was an appealing move for both personal and vocational reasons.

Unfortunately, Shari's drug use became obsessive as her grip on reality declined. Our relationship became vitriolic. I could find no explanation for some of her actions. Once, she hit herself in the face repeatedly and then filed charges against me for battery. Later, she got an injunction against me, which prevented me from seeing Robert and Aliea for six months.

My meth use was off the charts. I stayed up for up to a week at a time, ostensibly because I needed the time and energy to solve my marital problems. But the drug became my replacement wife. It also helped cover my legal fees while I was fighting for custody of my kids. Now I was selling meth, both to raise money and to support my own habit. I sold my bikes and everything else I could get a few dollars for.

At age 32, I was no less ugly or self-centered than I'd been at age 16. Only now I had the meth-monkey on my back as well. By this time, few of my friends would have anything to do with me.

Shari and I eventually agreed that Aliea would stay with her and Robert would live with me. We agreed not to make any child-support arrangements.

I took Robert and moved to Daytona, fully intending to make a fresh start. I got a job at Kmart as a receiving clerk and made the usual resolutions about saving money, etc. However, I couldn't stay away from meth. My new and improved life was kept perpetually on hold as I made weekly runs back to Avon Park to score my supply.

Our living situation was a disaster waiting to happen. We stayed with a couple whose relationship was on the rocks. I came home from work one day to find the place in shambles — smashed lamps, overturned tables and blood splattered on the walls.

"We're leaving, son," I told Robert after cleaning up

the mess. I hastily gathered our belongings and called my friend Louise who came to pick us up, probably anticipating the opportunity to join me in my meth frenzy. I spent the next two months loaded to the gills, trying to forget the ruin my life had become.

King Richard had become a pauper. I was enslaved to a peculiar white powder, homeless, my family fractured, with no more possessions than could fit into a large Hefty bag. I knew I had completely failed my son.

Although I was borderline psychotic, I picked up the phone to ask for help.

Mike was my best friend, a 30-something biker who lived in Pennsylvania. To this day, I have no recollection of calling him.

The only thing I remember was walking outside to see a beat-up old pickup truck out front. A skinny guy named Skip climbed out and walked up to me.

"Are you Richard Fallon?" he asked without preamble.

"Yes."

"Go in the house, and get your things. You and Robert are coming with me."

"What are you talking about?" I laughed. "I've never seen you before in my life."

"Just get your things. Mike Krause received your phone call yesterday. You told him that if he didn't get you out of Florida within the next couple of days, you'd be dead. He sent me down here to get you and your son and bring you to Pennsylvania. Don't make me get physical. Just get your things, and get in the truck."

Lone Wolf Adoption

We arrived in Selinsgrove, Pennsylvania, 14 hours later. After a brief reunion, Mike took me aside.

"Okay, this is how it's going to be. You're staying with me now. Whatever you do, wherever you go, it all goes through me. We're going to get you clean."

I submitted to his control willingly, though I tested him initially. In the first place, my loss of functioning had punched a hole in my ego. Secondly, I had tremendous respect for Mike. He was one of those rare friends that you end up counting as family. He had often traveled to Florida so we could ride together. He was like a brother to me and an uncle to my son. And he had responded jackrabbit quick to a call for help I couldn't even remember placing.

During the time I lived with Mike, I looked after Robert, who was 7 years old and going to grade school. I attended recovery meetings, managed my affairs and rebuilt my life piece by piece.

Six months later, Mike helped me get into an apartment in Selinsgrove. Robert grew like a weed. As for me, my head hadn't been so clear for years. I started looking for work and quickly landed a job as a loss-prevention officer at Sears. I also joined the National Guard. While all this was going on, Mike kept regular tabs on me. He often told me, "Don't screw up. Remember, you're not the only one who'll pay for it."

☙☙☙

Dirty Little Secrets

Though I went through many tumultuous episodes in my life, I had a genius for reinventing myself. I have been a military man, a drug dealer, a thug, a professional manager, a motorcycle mechanic, a highly paid retail executive, an animal breeder and many other things. I have been like a chameleon all my life.

I was married briefly to my third wife, Rhonda, based largely on our shared interest in animal breeding. During a time when I was looking for structure, Rhonda was happy to give it. She was the maternal type, and though I was her husband, I felt more like her son. She kept control of the money and the major living arrangements. She was far more stable and prudent in her decision-making than I was. Moreover, I went along willingly with her decisions at the outset.

Rhonda and I made strong strides in the animal breeding business. For several years, we perfected our system, earned splendid sums of money and were even featured on Animal Planet. In the end, however, I couldn't take being kept under her control. Over time, Rhonda had tightened the constraints on my behavior to ludicrous proportions. I was not allowed to attend concerts, make simple cash expenditures or even drink a beer. We ultimately divorced in 2003.

❧❧❧

In the meantime, I resolved to change careers again and was hired as the national sales manager for a huge pet-products company. On my first day, I was introduced to 17 women, all of whom would report to me. During the course of that day, as I went around getting to know the people I would be managing, I entered one of the offices and greeted the two ladies there. One faced the doorway and returned my greeting. The other woman turned toward me as I entered.

I couldn't speak.

In my early 20s, I'd drawn a portrait of the "perfect" woman. I was so happy with the result that I had a tattoo artist render it on my bicep. Over the next 20 years, I thought less and less about the tattoo and the drawing that had inspired it. Until now. The woman — Lily — who turned around to answer my greeting looked exactly like the portrait I had drawn.

In an instant, I lost all my social skills. I backed out of the office babbling like a deranged man.

Lily thought I hated her. It took months of working in proximity with her to break the ice, so much did her perfection terrify me.

During my first weeks at the company, I regularly lost my composure with her. My knees knocked whenever we were alone together.

Eventually, I began to relax with her. We were together constantly, traveling from city to city selling pet supplies. Our work kept us in close quarters, where, at last, we began to click, more wonderfully than I could have imagined. I also learned she was a mom to three little boys.

One day, Lily came in to work, and I asked about her missing wedding band.

"Ken and I are getting a divorce," she said.

It doesn't seem right to gain one's soul mate through the provision of a failed marriage, but that is exactly what happened. However, it took proddings from several of my colleagues before I could even bring myself to approach her with a romantic overture. The word was that everyone in the building saw what was happening before I could even acknowledge the possibility. Apparently, that included Lily, because one day, as I stopped by her desk to confer with her, she turned to me and said in a calm, gentle voice, "Just so you know … you and I are going to be together."

Lily was much younger than I, extremely personable and the spitting image of my dream girl from so long ago. She was so desirable to me that she was positioned to accomplish what 40 years and the prayers of relatives had been unable to do.

In a strange twist, Lily's affection for me (which resulted in our exchanging wedding vows in 2010) caused an awakening of her long-dormant faith in God — the conviction that God is good, ever-watchful and never without grace and compassion for lost people. Those convictions began tumbling out of her mouth when we were alone together.

"This life isn't going to last forever," she told me. "There's something on the other side. You should prepare for it."

"Yeah, okay." I always changed the subject when she spoke about God. Lily was convincing, but it was a tough sell for me.

Ever since I was old enough to understand that my mother had been taken away from me because of a brain aneurysm, I had considered God my adversary, a being undeserving of respect, praise or loyalty. My bitterness against God was so strong that it overpowered considerations of my own eternal fate.

"I'm a soulless b******," I told her more than once. "My past is my armor. That's just the way it is."

But Lily was at once persistent and gentle.

Over time, her soft radiance worked its way underneath my anger. "One of these days, you'll get it," she said again and again. "And no matter what happens, I love you to death!"

While these kinds of exchanges were going on, we learned that my son, Robert, who was by now grown and in the military, would soon be returning home from overseas.

"You know how badly I want to see my son," I told Lily. "Maybe I should start putting out applications in Columbia." This was where my son would be living upon his return.

The first hit seemed like a winner: working for one of the Harley-Davidson dealerships in South Carolina. After an examination of my credentials, the general manager offered to fly me down for a lengthy interview.

I flew to Columbia and made the first trip to the

dealership. As I threaded my way through the city, I noticed a church set a good distance off the road. Then I took a second look.

For as long as I could remember, I had despised churches — both because they were associated with God and also because, as I saw it, most of them were loaded with what I called smarmy mealy mouths. However, I felt none of my characteristic vitriol as we drove past this one.

The church building was black with lime-green trim. I saw several prominent signs in front of the building with the famous Angry Birds drawings on them. It was a conspicuous way of informing passersby that they specialized in helping people deal with anger issues.

As I took all this in, I had a thought that was completely out of character for me: *Maybe this is a church Lily and I could go and check out sometime. Maybe I'm supposed to see what the place is about.*

But the strangest things were yet to come.

After we had been in Columbia for nearly a month, a salesman at the dealership came up to me at work and began a bizarre monologue out of the blue. It may be that the only reason I listened to Hector was because of Lily's patient encouragement and the sighting of the Angry Birds church.

"Richard," he began, "I don't know how long you're going to be at the dealership here. But I'm going to tell you something: I've been praying for you for a long time."

At this point, I inwardly debated whether I should politely excuse myself.

"I can assure you that you're exactly where you need to be. You're here for a reason. I don't know what that reason is, but I've observed you. I know you. And I'm here for you."

I didn't know what to say. My usual response to such gushings was to dismiss them out of hand. But something visceral held me there. I felt a trust for him that I couldn't explain or justify.

Several weeks later, the dealership (lobbied by Hector, among others) gave permission for an evangelism outreach to be held in the back lot. Tents were erected, loudspeakers were set up and flyers were distributed.

The evening arrived. Lily and the boys came for the event, and we stood surrounded by balloons listening to the meeting get underway.

About 20 minutes into the event, I began to feel bored and walked back to the building to discuss some work-related item with the manager. When I returned, it had begun to rain. Hector was speaking by this time, but instead of listening, I strode back toward the building again to get my motorcycle. I was heading home.

Then I stopped.

I don't remember what Hector said. All I remember is stopping dead in my tracks, which was odd because tent revivals were about number 762 on my list of things to do. Even more ironically, I was getting completely drenched as the rain produced a gentle roar on the asphalt and the tops of the tents.

I turned and began moving back toward the main tent

where Hector spoke. He was getting fired up now. His cheeks were wet.

Lily told me later that as she watched me do this confused dance from a hundred yards away, she saw the expression on my face completely change and my jaw drop.

I stood in the same spot with hardly a twitch while Hector spoke.

"... this is what it means to *belong*," he was saying. "Being there for other people isn't just something we do for *them*. We do it for ourselves at the same time, but not in a selfish way. A person who doesn't have someone to care for is like a finger or an arm cleaved away from the body. It is dying. Its life is spilling out. Left alone long enough, it is nothing but a slab of flesh. It can only live as a part of the body, and that means reaching out to help others."

Hector's words cut to my heart. I realized that I *was* that disembodied arm, putrid and dying. I had chosen to walk alone through life, probably in the aftermath of my mother's death. My estrangement from God, my self-reliance, my lifelong habit of bending everything to suit my own wishes — all of it had kept me in a famished state as I hopped from marriage to marriage, job to job, career to career. I saw the answer in an instant. All those years, I had taken pride in my lone wolf status even as it asphyxiated me.

Sometime later, Hector spotted me and came over. He looked me over solicitously for a moment.

"Are you all right?" he asked.

"Yeah, I'm fine," I replied. "You know what? I *get* it."

Hector smiled and nodded. "That's why you're here."

As Hector prompted me, while the wind sprayed warm rain all around, I stood there and gave my life to Jesus.

"Speak it aloud," Hector insisted. "Use your voice!"

"My life belongs to you, Lord! I'm sorry I stood away from you for so long. I was wrong. Don't let me be alone anymore!"

And he hasn't.

Hector recommended a church for me — the same one Lily and I attend today. It is, in fact, the very church I noticed on my first drive through Columbia — black and lime-green with Angry Birds on the signs.

I went into Vive Church for the first time wearing blue jeans, leather chaps, a Harley vest covered with patches and pins, short-sleeved t-shirt, bandana and my arms covered in tattoos. Never in all my life have I been received so warmly by people wearing suits and "civilian" clothes.

Those civilians have become my extended family. They helped me shake loose from my past. I am convinced it is never too late for anyone to make it back. No one is too far gone to be saved.

I was at one of those "tent revivals" at my church recently when a total stranger walked up to me wearing a huge grin.

"Hey, brother," the man said like we were old friends.

"I've been watching you all evening. You're going to have an impact on this world. Believe it!"

I believe it. The love of God and my association with the people at Vive Church have taught me that any of us can be a star. Not because of our talents, strength or charisma, but because of Jesus.

Beauty for Ashes
The Story of Lily
Written by Arlene Showalter

Peace at last. I settled into the hushed silence of our local library. *No mean boys. No snickering girls. No parents. No rules. No frowning God.*

Just books and me. I smiled inside as I reached for the latest book in the *Sweet Valley High* series, eager to shed my dull existence and leap into the lives of twins Elizabeth and Jessica. I sighed.

They possessed everything I longed for — beauty, popularity, tons of friends and exciting lives. Sometimes I switched over to *The Hardy Boys* series, reveling in the exhilarating adventures of the young heroic duo.

Reality receded as fantasy nourished my lonely, hungry heart.

ೞೞೞ

My parents worked as missionaries on the streets of Philadelphia. They set up a storefront church among what I considered the dregs of human society.

Our parents' denomination held high expectations, especially for "preacher's kids." No pants touched female legs, no makeup stained female faces. No movies. No fun.

We moved across the street from low-income housing projects when I was 11.

Dirty Little Secrets

Railroad tracks ran alongside them, on the other side of a low wall. My parents kept us behind a locked gate, and Mom homeschooled us.

We stared out at the hostile environment beyond the gate, while kids stood on the other side, laughing and pointing at us.

We thought the drug addicts and homeless my parents helped were freaks. The neighbor kids thought the same about us.

"Why do you dress so stupid?" one girl asked, pointing at my culottes. "You look weird."

"Well, you're going to hell if you don't get saved," I retorted.

To escape the strict rules of home and taunts of neighborhood children, I'd go to the library two blocks from home. Silent books surrounded me, rather than smelly homeless, crazy addicts or judgmental church members.

I lost myself in another world, one of beautiful girls, nice boys and filled with excitement and fulfillment.

The short walk home proved as hazardous as a minefield. Kids from the neighborhood rode by and slapped me. Others tried to yank my culottes down to my knees.

"You better watch out, because you're going to hell," I warned the girl blocking my path.

"I talked to my priest. He says *you're* the one from the devil, so just shut your mouth before I slap it off."

Beauty for Ashes

Kids threw rocks against my bedroom window. They spray painted *the devil's gonna get you* on the side of our house.

This is the reward for serving God?

☙☙☙

My parents sent me to a Christian camp when I was 13, and the girls there wore makeup and pants. The girls sized me up and down, my hairy legs and culottes, and giggled behind nail-painted hands.

While the other girls dressed for swimming, I pulled a t-shirt over my bathing suit. They stared at me. *Even in a "Christian" camp, I'm the odd duck. I can't believe what these girls get away with. They even swim when the boys do!*

I turned away from their twittering excitement.

Mom let me attend Christian school in ninth grade. I found one friend among all the mocking kids. Totally Goth Ginger, with safety pins in her ears, saw past my different clothing and invited me into her circle. She challenged all boundaries, but I hesitated — for a while.

Ginger lived with her grandmother, and sometimes I stayed over. She lent me short shorts, which I hid under my clothes, and we snuck out of the house after Grandma retired for the night.

Ginger introduced me to her hard-living crowd where I experienced the first miracle of my life. They accepted me. So I embraced their lifestyle. *I belong. At last, at 14, I belong!*

"This is Zach." Ginger introduced me to the hunk leaning against a wall with loosely crossed arms.

"Hey, gorgeous."

Wow. Zach's 22, and he thinks I'm beautiful.

"Can I kiss you?"

I melted into him. Dark thoughts penetrated my bliss. *This is wrong. But it feels so good. It's still wrong.*

"I can't do this." I pushed Zach away and stared at his feet.

"Why not? This is what boyfriends and girlfriends do." He lifted my chin with a single finger. "Don't you want to be my girlfriend?"

I nodded. As our lips locked again, he slipped his hand in my pants.

"I can't."

"Fine." He shrugged and walked away.

I watched his departing back with clenched fists.

Will I ever be loved?

"Can I see you?" Zach called me a few months later.

"Okay." *He still likes me!*

"Saturday."

"Park down the street. I'll have to wait until my parents go to sleep."

"Sure 'nuff, gorgeous."

☙☙☙

"My life sucks," I said as we spun away in his white Corsica.

"It won't tonight. So, tell me, where do the local kids hang out?"

He handed me a cigarette. *This is so cool.* I rested against the seat and inhaled. "The woods in the park. Turn right at this corner."

He started kissing me as we approached the tree line. I pulled back a little. I knew all about a certain mattress that lay on one side of the trail that got more action than one in a Motel 6.

Zach kissed me deeper. "There's nothing to be afraid of. You'll feel so good. I promise."

We took a walk, and then he pushed me down on that nasty mattress. "This is what boyfriends and girlfriends do."

I tried to get up. "I can't." He reminded me of the rough gang he ran with.

I froze. *He could stab me like those women on the news.*

He finished what he'd set out to do. *What just happened?* I studied the ground as a tidal wave of shame washed over me. "Please take me home."

My body, soul and spirit ached as I went through the motions of playing the piano and singing for the church service the next day.

Four days later, I hung out with my bad-a** friends, trying to forget.

"Let me have a drag of that." I held out my hand to a

cute boy with a cigarette. His two buddies flanked him.

"Sure thing. You wanna go for a spin in our car?"

I looked at the one he pointed out. *Wow, is that ever cool.*

The three escorted me. *I'm going to miss curfew. What the h***.* I felt so included — a rarity in my life. *I'll deal with it when I get home.*

My body trembled as the driver pulled next to the same woods where Zach had assaulted me. *Oh, no! This is not what I expected.* The three guys tumbled out. One yanked open my door and grabbed my wrist.

"Come on, baby. We're in need of some sweet comfort."

I pulled back. He leaned in, and his eyes bored into me.

"Listen up, b****. We got us mob connections. You so much as squeak and we'll have you wasted."

They dragged me to the same mattress where Zach had done his thing with me, and they tossed me on it like I was a limp Raggedy Ann doll.

It's my fault, I thought, turning my head away from the nightmare. *This is God's punishment for what I let Zach do to me.*

"What's wrong with you?" Mom asked when I returned, late and dirty. "Why are you so pale?"

"I was running in the woods. I lost my watch."

She stepped closer. "I smell cigarettes."

"Wasn't me," I lied. "I ran into a friend who tried to help me find the watch. She was smoking."

Beauty for Ashes

What the h*** is wrong with her? I stared at my pale face in our bathroom mirror. *Why can't she see past my lies? Why didn't Mom push to get the truth out of me? Does God care? He knows the truth. Why doesn't he talk to them?* Shame wrapped itself around my heart like a hungry boa constrictor. *God will never forgive me for all the lies, sneaking around and now sex.*

A wailing sound announced an approaching train. *It would be wonderful to lay my body across those tracks and end it all in one swift moment.*

༓༓༓

"We're going to Florida," Dad told me, not long after the rapes. "For a church convention. And you're going, too."

"I'm 15. I don't want to go."

"We can't trust you. No telling what you'd do while we're gone," Mom said. "You might even try to run away."

We went. The preacher drove a nice car, and his family lived in a big, beautiful house.

What's wrong with us? We live next to the projects, and Mom shops at thrift stores. This sucks. I'm sick of poverty, secondhand clothing and my whole dowdy, miserable life. How can my dad preach about your goodness when my life is a living hell? This is our reward for serving you, God?

Dirty Little Secrets

I went to a different Christian school for 11th grade. The high school was farther from home than the last one, so my parents let me stay with Hanna, a new Christian friend who lived closer to school and attended the school's church. My parents liked that their family observed the same rules. Even while living with them, I continued sneaking out and lying.

I became interested in medicine at a young age, so I applied for Emergency Medical Training (EMT) when I was 17 and still in high school.

Near the end of my EMT training, a call came in, and I accompanied the crew. We arrived at the scene and found dead animals lying around. A man had shot his pets before blowing his own brains out.

We couldn't move anything until police arrived, to be 100 percent sure it was a suicide and not a homicide. I stood around for hours, my eyes and brain trying to process the gory scene. Rigor mortis had set in. I helped put the man's stiff remains in a body bag.

"You want a ride home?" Kyle, one of the other EMTs, asked.

"Thank you. I appreciate it."

The moment he pulled up to Hanna's house, their front door flew open.

"We're sick of your sneaking and lying," Hanna's father said, glaring at Kyle's car as it disappeared around the corner.

I leaned against the porch rail to quiet my shaking body. "I wasn't sneaking. I was out on a call."

Beauty for Ashes

"You're lying."

I bit my lip to keep tears in check. "It's the truth."

"We don't believe you. You can't stay here anymore."

This is great, God. These "Christians" are supposed to hear you. Why didn't you bother to tell them I spoke the truth?

❧❧❧

"We're moving upstate," Mom announced, two months before my 18th birthday.

"I don't want to go."

"You're still 17 and living under our rules," Dad said. "We've caught you in too many lies and can't trust you to live elsewhere. You're going."

We moved from Philadelphia to a mountain town where bears outnumbered cops.

I located the wrong crowd in no time, became friends with Becky and further perfected my ability to sneak out without my parents' knowledge.

"My friend's having a bash," Becky told me, five months after our move. "Wanna go?"

"You bet."

I inhaled jungle shots, while the party escalated out of control. Neighbors called the police. Another kid and I dashed into the woods to hide just as the police cars arrived.

"Where have you been?" Dad demanded when I returned home, wasted and reeking. "Don't bother to lie your way out of this. You don't think I know a hangover when I see one?"

"How can you play for service tomorrow?" Mom asked.

I saw double notes, double Dad, double Mom and double congregation as I stumbled through the music at the piano the next day.

"I'm so disappointed in you," Mom cried when we got home.

"I don't care!" I screamed back. "I hate it here. You forced me to move. I'm 18 now, and you can't make me live like this anymore. I'm leaving — today."

I moved in with Becky and plunged into the party lifestyle. What boys had taken in rape I now freely gave. *May as well give before they take.*

I took a job at a bar and reveled in the attention I got from the men there. I dangled my body and took what I could get. I strung my conquests like a string of popped corn. The tips piled up.

"Here's the deal, Lily," my boss said. "We're going to give you a room upstairs to service the men. Take it or get out."

I got out. And went home.

"You can't stay here and do what you're doing," Dad said. "This is a small town. We know all about your reputation."

"You have to live by our rules," Mom added. "You need to have more respect for yourself. You need forgiveness and a fresh start."

I tried. Dad bought bags and bags of Skittles to help me get over the sugar cravings I developed while trying to quit alcohol. *They've done so much for me. I have to get my act together. They don't deserve this pain.*

But soon after I thought I'd recovered, I returned to my old ways. Got caught. Got lectured about the rules. Tried again. Rebelled. The cycle continued.

Mom's sister, Lucy, who lived four hours away, offered to take me in.

"All Lily needs is a fresh start."

I found a job at Red Lobster and began saving my money. Lucy and I got along great. Then she invited Jake to move in, a guy she'd met at work. He was on a work-release program.

"You spend too much money on that brat." Jake glared at me through drink-reddened eyes.

"She's my niece."

Night after night, I lay in my bed, shaking worse than any alcohol detox, and listened to Aunt Lucy pacing the floor, waiting for Jake to come home from the bar.

I came home from work one day and went straight to my bedroom — the only refuge I had in the house. I heard Jake's heavy steps come toward my door. He kicked it open.

"You have to f****** move!" He turned and started down the basement steps. "You're a pain in my a**."

Aunt Lucy shot from her bedroom. "Don't you talk to her that way." Jake spun around and barreled up the steps, slamming into Lucy. Her body sailed in the air, and she landed hard, hitting her head.

"I'm sorry, baby." Jake knelt over her as she lay, moaning. "I'm so sorry. I thought you was *her.*"

I can't leave her! She needs my help. But I can't stay! He'll kill me. Finally, I leaped over their bodies, grabbed the cordless phone and ran into the yard, punching 911.

A neighbor passed the house, walking his dog, while I babbled incoherently. The police came. I finally choked out my story so they could understand me.

"She telling the truth?" The officer turned to Jake.

"Yeah."

They hauled him off to jail and called for an ambulance to tend to Aunt Lucy's concussion.

"What are you going to do?" I asked Aunt Lucy. "The police can only keep Jake a month unless you press charges."

"I'm not going to," she said. "He wants to come back, and I've decided to let him."

ം ം ം

What can I do? My fingers trembled as I logged onto the Internet. *I can't go back home. I hate it there. I can't stay here. Jake will kill me.*

I had met Dave online, and now desperation kicked in. I needed him. *Let's meet,* I typed. We decided on the local Wendy's restaurant and both experienced lust at first sight. We checked into a motel.

"Let's see how far our chemistry goes," I said, putting it all out there. "Can I move in with you?" *A move will put three hours between Jake and me.*

I got a job working at the same mill as Dave. Besides sex, we shared a love of music. I'd learned to play at a young age and had led the music for Dad's church. Our family also sang together, one of the bright spots in my life. Music took me to a wonderful, pure and peaceful place.

Nobody's ever shown a flicker of interest in my music before. How cool it is to compose and sing music together.

But I soon tired of Dave. He was too hippie, too New Age, too vegan and too old for me. I was ready to move on.

ช่ช่ช่

I met Ken at work. He always carried a wad of bills from his side business dealing illegal drugs, and, oh, how his money talked to me. We struck up a friendship that quickly merged into a physical relationship.

"It's silly to pay for two rents," Ken said. "How about you move in with me?"

"Works for me." I did, and we married two months later.

We became the "beautiful couple" at the local clubs where Ken dealt and used. Then I got pregnant. *Fantastic! At least I'm not one of those tramps who gets knocked up out of wedlock.*

Dirty Little Secrets

We both welcomed the new life growing inside of me. I purchased a single white sleeper to focus on the coming joy rather than horrific morning sickness. My mother-in-law bought a bassinette, and soon, she had it piled high with baby items.

At 16 weeks, I went in for an ultrasound. The doctor scowled at the paper ribbon of data the machine spit out.

"There's no heartbeat." He lifted the paper strip high. "See? Your baby's dead."

Ken began crying. I turned my head away. *This is you, God. The only time you ever show up in my life is to punish me.*

We called his mom with the sad news. "I told you not to buy baby things too soon," she told me. "See? It's your fault."

But didn't she buy all those things in the first place?

After I lost the baby, I became anxious. I gained weight. Lost weight. Doctors gave me medications for depression.

"You need to snap out of this," Ken said months later. "Mom says it's all in your head."

"Lactating for no reason is all in my head?" Later, I learned this was a medical side effect to the antidepressant medications prescribed for me.

He shrugged. "I agree. I think it's all in your head."

I got off the medications and stabilized. The mill closed down. I stayed home, and Ken got a better job.

Then I got pregnant again, and in October 2003, I delivered a healthy boy, Robbie.

Beauty for Ashes

A few months later, we attended a friend's Christmas party. "Time to go," Ken said, stumbling to our Neon. I clutched my newborn close.

"You're drunk. I'm not getting in."

Ken slammed the car into drive and scraped it hard against his buddy's truck. He stopped and rolled down the window. "Get in," he ordered. "If you don't, I'm not coming back for you."

I clung to the seat with both hands. *God, save us. Please save us.*

"Where did this come from?" Ken pointed to the long scratch along the side of the Neon.

"You hit that truck at the party."

"Did not."

"Call your friends, and ask them."

They confirmed my story.

"You need to talk to Ken," I sobbed to his mother. "He drinks so much."

"He wouldn't need to if you treated him right."

I took a job at a pet-products warehouse as a packer in 2004. And got pregnant again. When I was in my third trimester, our department got a new boss. A big, burly guy named Richard.

"Quack, quack. Waddle, waddle," Richard sang as I passed his office.

I rolled my eyes. *He's so annoying. Typical male. No clue how it feels to be eight months pregnant. Cripes, I miss our old boss.*

"I'm going to sleep in the baby's room," I informed Ken shortly after Josh's birth. I left his bed and my wedding rings behind.

Six weeks later, I sat nibbling on pretzels. Sudden pain slammed into me, and I doubled over.

I went to internists. One diagnosed kidney stones. Another, a hiatal hernia. The pain continued, and blinding headaches followed.

Months passed with no definitive answers, only frightening potential diagnoses, such as cancer and blindness. I sat on my front porch one day, anxious and alone. Ken came outside and started down the steps. He turned at the last one and looked up at me.

"Mom says it's all in your head." He spun around and headed for his car. "I agree with her."

I stared at him. *How many times has she accused me of everything being in my head?* I pushed myself up out of the chair.

That's it. I'm done.

Ken worked night shift, and I worked during the day, so it was easy to avoid one another. I got another promotion and lingered at work to stay away from the beautiful house that Ken's wad of money had purchased. That wad also bought nice furniture, cars and clothes.

However, it failed to provide love.

My promotion brought me in direct contact with Richard. We often drove together to area stores to check product.

An easy friendship developed. I felt safe with Richard. Even though technically married to Ken, I started flirting with the also-unhappily-married Richard.

The relationship took an even more inappropriate turn when we stood, alone, on the second floor of another store.

"You going to kiss me or not?" I teased. *Let's see what it feels like.*

Richard obliged.

That felt good. Guilt set in. *I'm married. Richard's married. He's miserable with his wife. I can't stand Ken. Now what do we do?*

"Will you hang around a few minutes after work?" I asked Richard a few weeks later. "I want you to meet my boys."

Richard and I had begun calling one another for 100 percent non-work-related conversations. *I'm not sure where this is going, but I feel so easy around him,* I thought, as I drove to the daycare to pick up my sons and bring them back to work.

Richard met us in the parking lot.

"Wow, these are cool," 3-year-old Robbie said, running his hands up and down Richard's tattooed arms. "Can I color them, too?"

"'Fraid not, buddy." Richard laughed and ruffled Robbie's hair. Robbie continued studying each tattoo and discovered one peeking out from the edge of Richard's short sleeve. He pushed the sleeve up.

"Why you have a picture of Mommy on your arm?"

Richard jerked the sleeve down and turned red.

"What does he mean?" I asked.

He rolled the sleeve back up, exposing a woman who looked … just like *me*.

That's kinda sweet. Wait a minute — he must like me more than he's let on, I thought, gasping.

He shrugged. "Had that put there almost 30 years ago. My ideal woman." He grinned.

"Okay, boys, I think it's time to go," I stammered as I clutched baby Josh closer and hustled Robbie into his car seat.

"I'm going to listen to a band this Friday," I told Ken, naming a place an hour away. "I'll be staying overnight with my friend."

Richard met me at the bar where the band would play. I loved the music.

"Come on, let's dance." I dirty-danced against him, displaying all the sleazy moves I'd learned back in the hills of Pennsylvania.

Later, we drove to his house.

"What about your wife?"

"She's gone to a dog show this weekend."

Richard led me down the hall and stopped at a door. "Here's our guest room."

"Please don't leave me." I pressed up against him.

"I have to meet my wife at the show today," Richard said the next morning.

I followed him into their kitchen. "I had decided to leave Ken even before last night," I said. "I think we have mutual feelings for each other."

Richard nodded.

"Neither of us deserves to be a side dish," I continued, "so until you decide what to do about your marriage, an affair is off the table."

"I've found somebody else," I announced to Ken the next day when I returned home. "As soon as I can find a place to live, I'm leaving you."

"Why?"

"You know darn well why. Your mother will always be first in your life. I've tried to get you to understand how unhappy I am, but you ignore me. I tried to get us to move, for a fresh start for us both, and you said no to that, too. You think I'm crazy. That I invent pain for attention. You agree with anything your mother says about me. I'm done."

I found an apartment for the boys and me. Richard came for a visit.

"You can't live here alone. This area is too unsafe."

"So what're you going to do about it?"

"I'm moving in. The wife found your phone number and threw me out."

I smiled. *I'm safe.*

Then Richard lost his job. He couldn't find another, so we moved in with his friend, who lived an hour away, but his lack of employment soon led to fighting. I left and got an apartment. Even though I drove a battered car and slept on a mattress on the floor, I felt more independent than ever before.

But I missed Richard.

"Can you come over?"

"Sure, baby."

We both hugged and cried.

"I don't want to be without you," I said.

"I still haven't found work, but another buddy said we can stay there."

"I'll have to give up my job," I said. "How can we make it?"

"They said they'll pay for you to keep house. We'll pool our resources."

Richard finally found a job, which allowed us to move into our own place, and I signed up at the local technical school for training as an operating room assistant. The schoolwork challenged me, and I thrived on it.

I met a younger girl, Joy, at school. Her bright red hair and ready smile made her a class favorite. We became inseparable.

"Your house is on the way to school," I said, soon after we met. "How about if I pick up my Little Sister?"

"Okay, Big Sister. That would be so cool."

"I met a guy at a party. We had a good time." Joy grinned as she climbed into my car. "If you know what I mean."

"A one-nighter?" I frowned. "Be careful, Joy. I've done plenty of those in my time. You don't want to end up with a jerk. If you get pregnant, you're stuck with him for life."

"I don't feel well," Joy said a few weeks later, while we sat in the school cafe. "I'm going to call my grandmother to take me home."

"Be careful," I called after her as she left. *She didn't say "have a nice day."* I frowned. *She always leaves me with "have a nice day."*

"I'll take Robbie to daycare," I told Richard the following Monday. Normally he watched both boys because he worked from home, but on this day he felt sick. I didn't want to burden him with both boys.

"Thanks, babe. I appreciate that."

I tucked Robbie into his car seat and drove over to Joy's. The moment I pulled up in front of her house, my gut told me something was wrong. I knocked on the door. No answer. *That's strange. She always texts me if she's not going to make it to class.* I opened the unlocked door. The house was empty. I moved about, calling her name.

I can't leave Robbie unattended for long. Torn between finding Joy and returning to the car, I tried once more.

"Joy?" Silence.

I went back to the car, drove Robbie to daycare and went on to school.

A short while later, I got called into the dean's office.

"Sit down, Lily." He guided me to a chair with a gentle touch on my elbow. "I have some hard news. Joy committed suicide today. The police found her body hanging from the deck early this morning."

"How could you do this to me?" I screamed at Joy as I drove home. "And you, too, God. How could you let this happen?"

I got drunk. Very, very drunk.

❧❧❧

Richard supported me through my grief over Joy's death and became the rock in my life that I'd never had before.

Then I got pregnant.

I stared at the telltale stick that announced, "Yes, dear, you are pregnant," and stomped through the house, looking for the culprit.

I found Richard in our room, talking to his boss on the phone.

"Thanks a lot, buddy," I snarled.

"What?" A blank look crossed his face. He turned back to the phone. "I'll call you right back."

Richard hung up and turned back to me. "What's going on?"

"You know how babies are made. But don't you worry. *Your* career won't be affected by this."

"We'll get through it, babe."

"Yeah, right."

I had to drop out of the operating room technician program because operations don't stop for morning sickness. I switched to clinical assistant.

Resentment, guilt and shame brewed in me. *This isn't the career I wanted. I'm a single mother, shacking up with a guy, and now I'm pregnant out of wedlock. Sure, we'd already planned to marry before I got pregnant, but a snowstorm kept Dad from coming to perform the ceremony, so here I am, single and pregnant. What would all those perfect churchgoers think about me now?*

We married a month later, in the office of the justice of the peace.

❦❦❦

Our neighbor Grace and Richard's son witnessed the three-minute ceremony, while Grace's husband, Stan, watched my boys. Stan and Grace demonstrated Christianity as neither Richard nor I had experienced before. They welcomed us as equals, even when Richard and I shacked up together. Neither recoiled when they saw Richard's extensive artwork of tattoos running up both arms and down his legs.

Over the years, my heart had softened toward my parents and Jesus.

As I juggled work and the children's snotty noses and skinned knees, I realized what a tough job Mom had had with her five.

This is life, I thought, as I struggled to pay another utility bill. *It's not God's punishment that I'm short of money.*

Ever so gently, God wooed me back to him. Stan and

Grace helped me grow in faith. When faced with any need, I told Richard, "We need to pray about this."

"Why? Where was God when my mom died?"

"He was with you, babe, just like he was with me when those boys raped me."

The doctors were concerned as they prepared me for a cesarean section because of my severe anemia. Allen's position forced them to keep the incision open longer than usual, and I lost a lot of blood.

Months later, I still hadn't recovered from the birth. Unbearable pain just wouldn't let up.

"You're just post-partum," one doctor told me.

"It's all in your head," another insisted, echoing Ken's mother's accusations of the past.

One diagnosed me with IBS (Irritable Bowel Syndrome). I dropped to 103 pounds.

Do I really belong to you, God? I felt close to death and wrote out a will. *What will happen to my sons? Richard? Will he ever turn to you?*

Finally, one doctor tested me for Celiac Disease, a condition in which the body develops a high intolerance to gluten — a substance found in many food products.

Though relieved to have a firm diagnosis after years of seeking, living gluten-free provided its own challenges. The merest smidge of gluten sends my body into turmoil for days.

Richard and the boys quickly learned to surround Mommy like anti-gluten bodyguards.

"Is that gluten-free?" Josh demanded, when a server brought my plate at a restaurant.

"Goo-tin fee?" Allen echoed.

These guys are my rock!

☙☙☙

Richard lost another job and started job hunting again. His phone rang.

He talked, then hung up and turned to me. Wonderment shone in his eyes.

"That was from a guy from that motorcycle dealership down in Columbia, South Carolina," he said.

"That's God!" I said.

"Let's keep God out of it." He scowled a little, then smiled. "They want to fly me down for an interview. Can you believe it?"

"It's God," I insisted.

"Whatever," he said, shrugging.

He flew down and stayed with his son who lived in the area.

"I got the job." He paused. "Guess what? I found a church."

What? Mr. you-will-never-see-me-darken-the-doors-of-some-hypocrite-hideout just said he found a church?

"It's really cool, painted all black with lime-green trim. Called Vive Church. And …" He chuckled. "They've got Angry Birds out front."

A peace settled over me. *This is God.* "Sounds good," I said.

"Want me to start looking for a place to live?"

"Yes!"

My body was energized, and I packed up our entire house for the move, which we made over the Easter break.

☙☙☙

The dealership allowed a Christian group to host *Rock the Lot* in its parking lot. Worship music was played, and several men spoke of everyone's need for God.

I glanced at the sky. The clouds looked ready to burst at any moment. *If it rains, Richard will leave. He won't hear your message of grace.* I lifted my hands. "Hold back the rain, Lord. Hold it off, and show my husband your real power."

At that moment, the clouds parted, and the sun struggled to shine. People pointed. *You heard my prayer, Lord.* The service went on. *You've shown yourself, not only to my husband and these people here, but to my heart as well.* God's peace flooded over me, and I took it as a sign he'd forgiven every single bad decision I'd ever made. All my doubts and fears over my relationship with God vanished.

Then the downpour began. I decided to get some chicken wings for the boys at a nearby restaurant.

"We'll leave when the rain lets up," Richard said.

When we returned to the parking lot, the rain slowed

to a drizzle. Richard started walking toward his motorcycle. *He's leaving. He won't hear your words.*

I watched Richard stop in the rain, hesitate and begin walking toward his cycle again. He stopped again and then turned toward the tent, getting soaked all the while. My heart pounded. *He's hearing you, God. He's hearing you. Please open his heart to Jesus today.*

As his friend and co-worker Hector continued addressing the crowd and telling them about God's love, I watched Richard's shoulders sag. I knew in that moment he was yielding to God's call of love, repentance and forgiveness.

I ran over to him. He turned and grabbed me in a big bear hug. "I finally get it," he said. Tears flooded his eyes. "Now I realize how much I need Jesus."

Hector came over to where we stood. People flocked around us, thumping Richard on the back and welcoming him into God's family.

"Here's a list of area churches," he said, handing a slip of paper to Richard.

"Look!" Richard said. "Here's that church I told you about. Vive. That church that's painted black with lime-green trim. Remember?"

"The one with Angry Birds out front?" I asked.

"That's it. Let's go check it out."

"I'll be happy to go with you," Hector offered.

I dressed in a long gray skirt, while Richard seemed to expose every tattoo possible. As he held the door of Vive

Church open for me, I braced myself. *Here comes "seven shades of judgment."*

Instead, people surrounded us, smiling, talking, embracing. We moved on into the main gathering space where the worship team struck up its first song, "One Thing Remains," by Jesus Culture.

> *Your love never fails.*
> *It never gives up.*
> *It never runs out on me.*

I lost myself in the music. The beat. The words.

> *Your love never fails.*
> *It never gives up.*
> *It never runs out on me.*

Healing tears sprang from my eyes as God's total giving, endless love flowed over, around and in me.

Oh, God! You never gave up on me, even when I gave up on myself. You never left me, even when I ran from you. You've been calling me to come home for so long. I'm coming. I'm coming, God.

After the service, I glanced around. *Thank you for guiding us to a church home that shows the same love, compassion and acceptance as you. Thank you for bringing Richard home. I love you so much, Lord!*

He Was Always There
The Story of Tonya
Written by Susan Hill

I watched for the front door of our small house to swing open, waiting with a confusing combination of anticipation and dread. The youngest of seven children, I knew my father considered me his favorite. For reasons I still can't explain, he was my hero. Yet, as I awaited his arrival, an uneasy foreboding settled in my gut. Perhaps because every time he walked through the door, I feared for my mother's life.

☙☙☙

After his shift ended, Dad left the shipyard, walked across the street to the tavern and drank until he was drunk. Though he had been involved in multiple affairs, the most devastating relationship was with my mother's youngest sister. Mom was aware of the relationship, and tension permeated our home like a dense fog. Despite the circumstances, when he finally arrived home, a hot dinner waited for him. Most nights, something trivial triggered his fury. She wouldn't get his food to him fast enough, or he claimed his dinner was cold. The slightest irritation induced fury in him that wasn't satisfied until damage was done. He threw plates of food at her, leaped from his chair, grabbed her by the hair and dragged her back and forth across the house like a ragdoll. He punched her full throttle in the face while screaming, "I will kill you, woman!"

Fearing for my mother's life, I would run outside sobbing. The dogs had dug a hole where I always hid my small frame under the house. Lying on the cold ground, I peered up through the cracks in the floor as he smashed her head into the floor. On the most volatile nights, I peeked through the cracks to see the barrel of his handgun jammed into Mother's mouth. Tears streamed down her swelling face as she begged for her life. I heard him repeat over and over, "I will kill you. Do you understand me? I will kill you."

No matter how many times the scene unfolded, the sight of it made me cry so hard my nose bled. As I lay on the cool ground under the house, I felt a warm trickle of blood spill down my face. Soon I heard my father's footsteps. He crawled under the house and reached for me. "Tonya, I am sorry. Things got out of hand. I promise this won't happen again. Let's go in the house and get you cleaned up."

Once inside, I usually found my mother on her hands and knees scrubbing the kitchen floor with a toothbrush — a punishment inflicted upon her by my father.

Unfortunately, at a young age, I was already well acquainted with death, so the possibility of my mother dying didn't seem far-fetched. I'd already been present when three people died.

He Was Always There

❧ ❧ ❧

The first was my father's aunt, my great-aunt, who I called "Rich Annie." Every weekend, starting when I was 4, she bought me a new dress. She started the tradition as incentive for me to go to church with her on Sundays. Rich Annie likely knew I needed to get out of the house, and she may have been concerned about my religious upbringing. I didn't know anything about God and associated his name with a curse word. Still, I looked forward to going with her every week. One Sunday, as I sat next to her in the pew wearing my favorite red and pink floral dress, she hunched over, fell on top of me and died of a massive heart attack. I trembled as her lifeless body pressed into my small body and panicked when I saw urine streaming down the church pew. Several years passed before I darkened the door of a church again.

Just two years later, I visited my grandparents' house and was playing with my 4-year-old cousin. His mother, my aunt June, suffered from what I later understood to be schizophrenia and hadn't been out of bed all day. We went to check on her. When I squinted through the shadows in the dim room, something didn't seem right. She had committed suicide, overdosing on medication. Strangely, I remember feeling scared but not sad. As paramedics came, I recall playing by the fireplace with her son as they removed her body from my grandparents' home.

By the time I was 8, I'd figured out a way to spend time away from the house. My best friend, Karen, and I were in

Dirty Little Secrets

the same class, and her parents let me come stay every weekend. I looked forward to the visit all week long. One Sunday afternoon, Karen and I played in her yard. We were taking turns pushing each other on a push mower that we converted into a push toy. Her father, a truck driver, washed his truck, while her mother tended to the flowers. Karen's 2-year-old brother, Kenny, rode around the yard on his Big Wheel. He stopped and asked us to push him on the mower. "Mature" 8 year olds didn't want a 2-year-old nuisance around, and we told him as much.

"Kenny, you are dumb, and we don't want to play with you. Get away from us," we said.

"Fine," he said, "I don't want to play with you meanies, anyway."

As he spoke those words, he pedaled his Big Wheel as fast as he could down the driveway and into the road. I watched as he was struck by a car and dragged on the Big Wheel nearly a half-mile down the road. The horror of the accident was even worse than what I witnessed at home. At the hospital, we learned Kenny was dead. The image of his little body being dragged down the road haunted me. It triggered something deep in the recesses of my mind and initiated the onset of night terrors, which I still suffer from today.

☙☙☙

The next several years, the chaos continued at home. Routine beatings, verbal abuse, alcoholism and violence were common in my upbringing. Although never the direct victim, I bore the scars. At my mother's lowest points, she attempted suicide. Later, she claimed it was an accidental overdose, but even then I knew the truth. My short time on earth had already taught me that death was an imminent possibility, and I lived in constant anxiety that if my father didn't kill her, she might kill herself.

The year I turned 13, my father quit drinking. It was the best thing that could have happened to me. I don't know what made him quit, I never asked. I was just grateful he did. The beatings stopped, and for the first time, there was peace in our home. Although completely dysfunctional by then, we were as stable as possible. For the first time, I didn't fear for my mother's life.

Two weeks before my 15th birthday, I asked permission from my father to go to the swimming hole.

He asked, "Have you done all your homework?"

Up until that day, I had never lied to my father, but I really wanted to go swimming. "Yes, Daddy, I promise I have done all my homework."

He agreed to let me go, and I remember feeling guilty because I had always told my father the truth. Finally, my life was better than ever, and I had told him a lie. While I played at the swimming hole, my father suffered a massive heart attack and died. I became convinced my lie had killed him. Two of my aunts were dead, my best friend's little brother was dead and now my father.

My father's passing was especially difficult because the last year of his life had been our best. His death put financial pressure on our household, and my mother took on two jobs. With little supervision, I began to find my way out into the world and was already making poor choices. My mother found it hard to tell me no. Looking back, I can see she felt guilty for what I had gone through and tried to make it up to me by providing monetarily or letting me get away with things. I began staying out late and hanging with the wrong crowd.

    During high school, I met a guy named Bill, and we began dating. In 1989, I turned 18, and we married. My hope was to start my own family and have a stable home life. I looked forward to having children and wanted a fresh start. Just one week after we married, he hit me for the first time. My childhood nightmare had followed me to my new home, except now I was the recipient of the abuse.

    But I knew how to handle Bill, or so I thought. When he began to beat me, I showed affection to him, and he would oftentimes quit. After hitting me, he cried and said, "Tell me I am not a punk." I reassured him that he wasn't, and for a time he stopped. This continued for a year. By our first anniversary, I couldn't take it any longer. I packed a few belongings and left to stay with a girlfriend in the mountains of North Carolina.

    After staying in North Carolina for eight months, I went to Myrtle Beach for a weekend. While in Myrtle

Beach, I got a call from my roommate, Jenny, telling me I needed to come home.

"Tonya, you need to come back right away and deal with Bill. He is sitting across the street in his truck watching our house. I saw him there two days ago and thought he would leave. You have to go talk with him, because this is creeping me out."

Listening to her plead with me to come home, I realized despite our eight-month separation, we were still legally married. I would have to eventually have a discussion with him to pursue a divorce.

When I arrived, Bill sat waiting for me in his truck. At first, the conversation went well. He agreed we needed to file for divorce. Prior to our separation, we stayed with his mother, and he asked me to get my things from her home. He planned to move soon, and his mother wanted my belongings out of her house as soon as possible. He swayed me with his calm and amicable manner and offer to help get my belongings. As soon as I climbed in the truck and shut the door, I knew I had made a huge mistake. We drove to his mother's house, and as soon as we walked through the front door, he tried to have sex with me. When I refused him, he started to beat me. Once again, I played my cards, and as he hit me, I showed him affection.

"Tell me I am not a punk. Tell me I am not a chicken for beating on a woman," he pleaded.

I reassured him that he wasn't. He allowed me to get my belongings and agreed to drive me back to my friend's house. Once we climbed back in the truck, the arguing started again. His penetrating eyes mocked me, and he smirked and said, "You aren't going back to Jenny's house. In fact, you're never going back."

As we continued to argue, we had a physical altercation in the truck, hitting each other as he drove. He stopped the truck on a country road, dragged me from the vehicle and beat me until I was unable to defend myself. As I lay there exhausted from the beating, he raped me repeatedly. He stood over my limp body and wrapped his belt around my neck, choking me until I gasped for air. I pretended to be dead. I knew that if he didn't believe I was dead, he was going to continue beating me until I was.

He jumped in his truck, and I heard him back out. I lay totally still, hoping he believed he had killed me. He pulled away, and I stayed there trying to recover and gain enough strength to get up. I felt dizzy and disoriented. Face down in the dirt, I heard a vehicle approaching. I glanced up and saw his truck speeding toward me. He planned to run me over. My body experienced a rush of adrenaline, and I stumbled to my feet, gaining enough momentum to limp into the woods. Unfortunately, my body was in no shape for a foot race, and Bill quickly caught me.

I saw the look on his face and once again resorted to manipulation. "Bill, I love you, and I want to be with you. This isn't your fault. This is my fault. I've been a terrible wife. Let's start over. We could have a baby," I pleaded.

He took my hand and led me back to the truck, driving

to a local motel. In six hours, I had been beaten, raped, strangled with a belt, chased through the woods and nearly run over by a truck. Blood and mud caked my skin and clothing, and large pieces of wood and sticks dangled from my disheveled hair. As we walked into the hotel room, he made it clear he wanted to have sex.

My mind raced for excuses. "Oh, Bill, look at me. If this is a new beginning for us, at least let me get cleaned up first. I love you so much, honey. Let's do this right," I said. "I forgot my cigarettes in the truck. Will you go get them for me, while I take a shower?"

He agreed to go get the cigarettes, and I pretended to get in the shower. As soon as he left the motel room, I locked the deadbolt on the door and called 911. Although Bill was arrested for battery and kidnapping, he was not charged with rape because we were legally married. In 1989, in the State of South Carolina, a spouse couldn't be charged with rape. Our divorce became final later that year.

❧❧❧

After my divorce, I began to earn a reputation as a rounder. In fact, I became notorious for fighting. Admittedly, I experienced a sense of gratification from it. One night in 1991, I sat at a country juke joint with my best friends, Carl and Wayne, and my sister-in-law, Courtney. We got in a fight at the bar with a couple of guys, and Carl took a nasty blow to the head with a wrench. I knew the fight was far from over, but I wanted to take Courtney home for safety. After we dropped her off, we intended to return to the bar to finish what we started. Despite Courtney's pleading for us to stay at her house, we jumped in Carl's brand-new Mustang GT and headed back to the bar. Burgundy with silver ground effects, it ran faster than the wind. We sat at a stop sign debating about how fast it could go when Carl gunned it. The last thing I remember is hitting an embankment and hearing their screams. I yelled, "Please, God, I don't want to die!"

And then everything went black.

I don't know how much time had passed before I opened my eyes. I woke up mad, convinced Carl and Wayne left me passed out in the car and went back in the bar without me. Everything was pitch-black and eerily silent. I staggered out of the car, walked around the back of the vehicle and tripped over something in the highway. I reached down in the dark and felt a head full of hair. As I leaned over, I recognized Wayne. I knew he was dead. Still, I did not comprehend that we had wrecked. I started praying and screaming. As I prayed, I noticed a porch light in the distance through the dark woods.

I ran through the woods and finally reached the house. I knocked and knocked, but no one answered. In total desperation, I ran to the next house. Finally a woman answered the door and saw I was covered in blood. She called 911 and drove me back to the accident.

Upon arriving at the scene, the state trooper working

the wreck confirmed my two best friends were dead. The speedometer was stuck at 135 with nothing left of the car except for the passenger's front seat where I had been riding. Initially, the state trooper did not believe I had even been in the accident. After he put me in the ambulance and realized the extent of my injuries, he said, "I don't know why you are still alive. Your seatbelt should have cut your torso in half. It's almost as if God removed you from the car and put you back in after it hit the tree. Apparently, God still wants you to be alive for some reason. You need to figure out why."

෴෴෴

In the days following the wreck, I felt glad to be alive, and yet I didn't want to live. I kept asking myself, *Why did I live when my friends died?* I started experiencing panic attacks and feared people could read my mind. To numb my pain and survivor's guilt, I drank vodka straight out of the bottle and wouldn't quit until I was unconscious. A week after the wreck, I passed out in a mud hole in my mother's front yard and had to be carried in the house by my brother. At my mother's insistence, we left town for a while. She took me to Virginia where we stayed with family, and I dried out.

When we returned to my hometown, I was sober and clearer-headed than I had been in some time. I had been home about a week when I got a call from a guy I dated in high school. Donnie and I had been on and off since we were 15 years old. When I got back in town, we started dating and lived together for the next six years. I quit drinking, and we started attending church. I was looking for answers as to why I was alive, curious why God had spared my life.

In my first pregnancy, I found out I was carrying twins. I miscarried one and gave birth to the second child, but there were complications. Taylor underwent major surgery as soon as he was born, and we learned shortly after that he had cystic fibrosis. Despite the medical issues, Donnie and I were grateful to bring him home.

Only six weeks later, and knee deep in taking care of a sick infant, I became pregnant with my second set of twins. Again, there were problems. My sons Jake and Alex were born two months early. Jake thrived and did well, but Alex became gravely ill.

Day after day, I sat at the hospital praying that God would heal my son. I believed he would. I was a good person, going to church, and had been searching for answers about my faith for more than a year. Everyone said God would heal my son. Instead, he continued to get sicker and sicker. When he was 4 months old, the doctor told us that there was nothing more he could do for our son, and he felt it was medically unethical to keep him alive. In one last attempt to save him, we agreed for him to have surgery. He developed an infection that spiked his fever, and we were forced to make the decision to remove him from life support. I regret that decision to this day.

Alex's death made me furious with God. Why would

he let him suffer? Why did I ever get pregnant, just for him to live four months? Back at home, I had one healthy 4 month old and a 13 month old struggling with cystic fibrosis. The stress caused enormous strain on our marriage, and Donnie and I grew apart, eventually splitting up. After six years of sobriety, I turned once again to alcohol.

The heartaches in my life piled up, and every disappointment drove me further from God and everything I had wanted. I left the boys with Donnie and went on a two-week binge, drinking heavily again. It was then I first started using Valium and Xanax to numb my pain. I filled my pockets with pills, taking so many I couldn't remember what I was running from. I woke up with men I didn't know and couldn't remember going home with. I ended up in jail twice for fighting.

In 2000, I met Rick, and we married. After two miscarriages, I gave birth to a healthy baby boy. Rick became addicted to crack and was physically abusive, which ended our marriage. In 2004, my mother died unexpectedly of complications from gallbladder surgery. I hit rock bottom. I went from one abusive relationship to the next, at one point with a vicious man who stalked me so persistently I had to get restraining orders in three counties. Still, I continued making the same choices.

My next relationship was with a man I married while on the run from the police. After a shootout in our front yard, we ran off to Vegas to get married so I wouldn't be forced to testify against him. I lost three babies to miscarriage during this time. While pregnant with my youngest child, his father held me down and squirted bug spray in my mouth, trying to kill the baby and me both.

The next couple of years involved moves to different states, while I went from one dead-end relationship to another, continuing to look for one that offered stability. I started selling drugs just to get by. During this time, I started attending church on and off again, still looking for answers. In desperation, I recall going to the altar and falling face down. I sobbed and prayed, "God, if you are there, make yourself known to me. Where are you? I am so tired of living like this." I left, feeling nothing and doubting his existence. I even wondered if I might be possessed by demons.

༺✦✦✦༻

As time progressed, my illegal activities intensified, and I feared I might face serious criminal charges. Not wanting to go to jail, I took my two youngest boys, then 12 and 6, and fled to Texas. While there, I continued to be involved in illegal activities to survive. We lived from hotel to hotel and, on one occasion, ended up sleeping in the car. I told my young sons we were going camping so they didn't realize we were homeless.

One night I left my 12 year old at the hotel with friends and took my 6 year old with me to a Walmart parking lot where I joined four others engaging in illegal activities. When we came out of Walmart to split up the

He Was Always There

he let him suffer? Why did I ever get pregnant, just for him to live four months? Back at home, I had one healthy 4 month old and a 13 month old struggling with cystic fibrosis. The stress caused enormous strain on our marriage, and Donnie and I grew apart, eventually splitting up. After six years of sobriety, I turned once again to alcohol.

The heartaches in my life piled up, and every disappointment drove me further from God and everything I had wanted. I left the boys with Donnie and went on a two-week binge, drinking heavily again. It was then I first started using Valium and Xanax to numb my pain. I filled my pockets with pills, taking so many I couldn't remember what I was running from. I woke up with men I didn't know and couldn't remember going home with. I ended up in jail twice for fighting.

In 2000, I met Rick, and we married. After two miscarriages, I gave birth to a healthy baby boy. Rick became addicted to crack and was physically abusive, which ended our marriage. In 2004, my mother died unexpectedly of complications from gallbladder surgery. I hit rock bottom. I went from one abusive relationship to the next, at one point with a vicious man who stalked me so persistently I had to get restraining orders in three counties. Still, I continued making the same choices.

My next relationship was with a man I married while on the run from the police. After a shootout in our front yard, we ran off to Vegas to get married so I wouldn't be forced to testify against him. I lost three babies to miscarriage during this time. While pregnant with my youngest child, his father held me down and squirted bug spray in my mouth, trying to kill the baby and me both.

The next couple of years involved moves to different states, while I went from one dead-end relationship to another, continuing to look for one that offered stability. I started selling drugs just to get by. During this time, I started attending church on and off again, still looking for answers. In desperation, I recall going to the altar and falling face down. I sobbed and prayed, "God, if you are there, make yourself known to me. Where are you? I am so tired of living like this." I left, feeling nothing and doubting his existence. I even wondered if I might be possessed by demons.

☙☙☙

As time progressed, my illegal activities intensified, and I feared I might face serious criminal charges. Not wanting to go to jail, I took my two youngest boys, then 12 and 6, and fled to Texas. While there, I continued to be involved in illegal activities to survive. We lived from hotel to hotel and, on one occasion, ended up sleeping in the car. I told my young sons we were going camping so they didn't realize we were homeless.

One night I left my 12 year old at the hotel with friends and took my 6 year old with me to a Walmart parking lot where I joined four others engaging in illegal activities. When we came out of Walmart to split up the

He Was Always There

money, five police cars surrounded us. My stomach turned sour, and I began to shake. The officers put everyone in handcuffs except me. Over the next two hours, the police searched cars and made arrests. As my son and I sat in the truck, I looked in the rearview mirror and saw a 5-year-old boy sobbing in the car behind us as he watched his mother get handcuffed and frisked.

I rolled down the window. "Sir?" I asked the police officer. "Could we have permission to go sit with that boy?"

The officer said, "Yeah, I guess you can, but don't get too comfortable because before the night is over, you are going to be in handcuffs, too. Enjoy your son while you can."

My son and I got in the car with the boy, and I started to cry. The little boy looked at me. "Do you know how to pray?"

I sat in the front seat sobbing. "No, I don't believe God hears me."

He said, "I know how to pray, my grandma taught me. Just fold your hands and talk to God."

In a moment of total desperation, my eyes blinded by tears, I folded my hands and said, "God, please help me. I just want to go home to my kids tonight." Over and over again I prayed until it was almost a chant. "God, if you will please help me go home to my kids, I promise I will never turn my back on you again."

We waited for what seemed like an eternity. I heard a knock on the window, and the police officer motioned me out of the car. As I got out, the first words out of his mouth were, "Do you want to go home to your kids tonight?" He spoke the exact words I had prayed for the last hour. He looked at me and said, "Come write a statement, and you are free to go."

In that moment, I believed. I believed God had answered my prayer and spoken to me. I believed he was real. This was my moment after all those years I had begged him to make himself known. My time had finally come. God spoke to me through the police officer.

I called my sister, and she borrowed the money for us to leave Texas and come back home to South Carolina. Several months passed, and I was ready to look for a church home. I attended several places but each time felt there was still something missing.

When I met David, things took a new turn. He had recently stayed in a motel room with no television or phone. The only thing to do was read the Bible that was in the nightstand drawer. While reading, he found a verse that encouraged him to part ways with the girl he had been seeing. David met me soon after.

We felt as though God put us together. We decided to try something new for both of us — a relationship based on purity. We didn't have sex. We curbed our drinking together. And we began church shopping together.

When I walked into Vive Church, I knew I had found my church home. I came in a stranger and left a friend. Pastor Randy, his wife and the staff there have welcomed me and treated me in a way I had never experienced. The

He Was Always There

best part about Vive is that the members and staff are honest about their flaws. When I am there, I don't feel judged or ashamed, and no one looks down at me. I don't have to hide anything. All the members admit they are broken, we are broken, and all in need of Jesus Christ. It is a community where people get set free.

Not long after I started worshipping there, my son Jake and I were enjoying a casual afternoon together. As we pulled into a McDonald's parking lot, he asked, "Mom, why do you pray to God?"

I looked him in the eyes and smiled. "Because I know he hears me, and I know he will show me the way if I don't turn my back on him."

Sitting in the car talking with my son, I realized that my children are starting to see evidence of God's work in my life. I, too, sense that God is producing changes in me. It's a slow process, but those closest to me are taking notice. It brings me great joy to tell my kids about God. I don't pretend to know all the answers, but I believe God is working, and I am making progress.

As I continue to grow in my relationship with God and am surrounded by the unconditional love and support of Vive Church, I feel more comfortable sharing my story. Since becoming a member of the Vive community, I no longer feel alone. I sense God in my life, in the music I listen to, in my church home, and I believe he speaks to me.

I believe he was with me every step of my journey. Every time I felt scared, every time I slipped into addictions, every time I started a fight, he was there, patiently waiting to love me and work in my life. Now, when hard times come, I have a loving father to turn to. Someone who makes me feel alive again.

Free From Me
The Story of Scott and Connie
Written by Arlene Showalter

Scott entered the kitchen just as I finished wiping down the counters. "We'll have to talk about this later, but I just want to tell you I'm filing for divorce."

I'll never forget that moment.

It was 10 p.m., Wednesday, December 13, 2006.

I stood there in my nightgown.

Scott held a hand up. "I've already made up my mind. Nothing to discuss. I'm leaving — now."

❧❧❧

Scott

"Does your son play any sports?" The principal asked the question of my father during the intake interview, when my parents decided to enroll me in a Christian school in fourth grade.

"Baseball and football."

"I'm so sorry, we don't offer those sports." He turned to me. "How would you like to play soccer, Scott?"

"I'm willing to try any sport."

That first day on the field started a love affair that quickly developed into an obsession for me. Later, it robbed me of quality family time with my wife and children.

Dirty Little Secrets

"Buck-tooth Scotty."

A major overbite and gangly limbs made me a fair target for getting picked on by peers. Without even trying to be one, I qualified as the poster boy for a stereotypical dork.

"Yeah, I know I'm a dweeb." I turned personal hurt into self-effacing humor and becoming the class clown. I didn't care that the kids laughed at me as long as I set the stage for it. I became the funniest guy in school, and the kids flocked around me.

My parents provided a stable home environment for their children, and our friends enjoyed hanging out at our house. Vacations included grandparents, aunts, uncles and cousins. And I could count on my folks showing up at 99 percent of my soccer games.

My father always taught me to never judge a person by his or her skin color or culture. "Only judge people by their character." His attitude toward others opened up doors for more friendships than I would have otherwise experienced growing up in South Carolina.

"Dream big," Dad said. "Dream, not fantasize. Set realistic goals, and work toward them." Most importantly, he said, "Don't ever let anyone take your dreams away."

By the time I hit high school, braces had straightened my teeth, and I'd grown into my arms and legs, for the most part. I was still skinny, but self-doubt had dissipated, and I gained confidence.

I became well known in my county and in surrounding areas as a really good soccer player. Soccer became my life's food and breath as I matured. Nothing else came first — not jobs, church or even, later, my wife and children.

"Where were you last night?" asked Cathy, my girlfriend of three years. "I called your house, and your mom said you weren't home."

"I was out with my buddies. I don't have to report my every movement to you. I'm not your pet."

"I saw you talking to Becky in the hall." Cathy became more possessive of my time and attention as high school graduation approached.

"So what? I'm tired of being controlled by you. We're done."

After graduation, I hopped from one party to another, especially during my first year of college. A weird thing happened. Instead of me seeking girls out or waiting for the perfect moment to express my interest, they began seeking me out.

"Hey, Scott, you remember Mary Jane?"

"Sure. She's the cute chick from math class."

"She's interested in you."

"Cool."

We hooked up for one night and both moved on with our lives. Soon a whole string of girls just as committed to having fun without commitment sought me out.

I began college with new interests: girls, smoking, marijuana and booze.

Dirty Little Secrets

Right after my second semester of college ended, so did my college career. I'd refused to give up partying to study. The college coach told me if I didn't pull my GPA up to at least a 2.0 by the end of the second semester, I would lose my soccer scholarship. I saw the writing on the wall before the second semester was over.

I decided to sign up for the Air Force on delayed enlistment and make a career of the military.

Meantime, some buddies and I decided to go to Myrtle Beach at the same time as thousands of high school kids from around the state and beyond converged at the beach for a week of nonstop partying. I knew some of the kids in the groups.

"Hey, Hale," I said, striking up a conversation with one of the seniors. "How's it going?" I studied the kids around us as we chatted. My eyes settled on a petite brunette.

"Wow, that chick is hot. Nice legs."

"You want to meet her? She's my sister." Hale turned to the girl. "Hey, Connie, come here."

"This is Scott," he said when she stood next to him. "He's from Newton, too."

Connie

"Come meet your new brother," Mom said two days after my second birthday. "You can be Mommy's big girl and help me take care of Ricky."

Eighteen months later, another brother, Hale, arrived.

"Mommy really needs your help now, Connie."

Free From Me

Ricky screamed. A lot. Especially after spending time in the sun.

Dad lost himself in work, and Mom ping-ponged between a demanding, fussy toddler and a newborn.

I felt pretty much on my own, starting at 4 years old.

No matter how hard I tried, as I grew older, neither parent seemed to take note of my achievements, only my flaws. Like when I'd hand my report card to Dad. His eyes would flick over the steady column of As and stop at the single B. He'd point to the one less-than-perfect mark. "What happened?"

I'd stare at my feet. *Doesn't matter what I do, I'll never be good enough. I have to try harder. Dad's got too many other things to worry about.*

"My hands burn. My feet burn," 6-year-old Ricky screamed during our vacation at a nearby lake.

Mom took blankets and layered them on the floor. Then she set bowls of ice water at the four corners for Ricky to stick his hands and feet in. Only then could he fall asleep.

Later, the doctors finally diagnosed his condition as Erythropoietic Protoporphyria, or EPP, a blood disorder that makes the individual extremely sensitive to sunlight. This helped us to understand his physical pain but not Ricky's aggressive behavior.

Later, other doctors diagnosed him with Bipolar Disorder.

"What's wrong?" I had just finished cutting Ricky's hair on the back porch, and he scowled in the mirror. He turned, and that all-too-familiar I'm-going-to-kill-you expression saturated his 12-year-old face.

I dashed inside, but he caught me moments later and began bashing my head on the corner of the kitchen cabinet.

Another time, he dried the dishes as I washed them. "You're not finished with that pot yet?" I asked as I prepared to hand over a dripping plate. *The Look* hit his face, and I took off, running down our long hallway. Dad intercepted us and tackled Ricky. Both crashed through the sheetrock wall.

Ninety percent of the conflicts in the house were between Dad and Ricky. In junior high, they got into a fistfight in the kitchen. Mom tried to separate them and got knocked to the floor.

"Come on, Mom," I urged as Hale and I got her to her feet and away from the fracas. I listened to the thumping and yelling coming from the kitchen.

This is my life. How I wish I could leave this havoc behind. But how? Besides, Mom needs protection from Ricky.

"Fatty, fatty, two-by-four. Can't get through the bathroom door." Home-grown stress caused me to comfort myself by eating. I began gaining weight in the third grade and widened with each passing year.

The boys' taunts hurt, but the girls' rejection hurt even

more. I lost myself in my greatest strength, schoolwork.

I sat at the top of the academic pile and the bottom of the social ladder. I decided to melt away some poundage and began looking, but not feeling, half decent by the time I reached my senior year.

In a small town, there's little to do except "cruise Main." The high school kids got together every Friday, Saturday and Sunday night to drive through the main part of town, talk to friends and meet new people.

On one such cruise, I met Ted. Eighteen inches taller than I, a poor student and a year younger, we became the quintessential odd couple.

I met him through my friend Cindy, whom he dated a few times.

"I'd really rather be going out with you," he confided.

"Well, here's the deal," I said. "I have to call her and ask if she minds because she's my friend. Are you okay with that? Because if you're not, I'm just saying no right now. Understood?"

He shrugged. "I don't have a problem with that."

Cindy granted permission and then changed her mind after Ted and I went out. She treated me with undisguised hatred.

My parents separated shortly after my high school graduation and later divorced. It devastated me. I went off to college about three hours from home, coming home when I could to see Ted.

I'd have been smarter to stay on campus. My academic

intelligence didn't help me exercise practical wisdom when Ted pushed for sex or when he took up drinking and began getting violent with me, much like my brother Ricky. Yet, I stayed with him.

I went home one January to celebrate Ricky's and my birthdays, being two days apart. Our family tradition was to all go out to dinner together, and my parents had promised they would get along for the evening. We took one car and drove to Charlotte, about an hour away.

I acted normal throughout the meal, but on the way home, I stared at the passing street lights and chewed on my inner lip. *I can't believe I'm pregnant. How can I tell Mom and Dad? Abortion's not an option.*

Suddenly a fight erupted between my parents — something I rarely saw in the years they occupied the same house. They had simply led separate lives. When Dad dropped Mom off at her own car, he yelled, "You shouldn't be surprised if Connie drops out of college or Ricky has to go back to drug rehab or Connie even gets pregnant, because it'll all be your fault."

Mom jumped out of his car and into her own, choking on her own tears.

They can't ever know, I decided.

"I can't keep this baby," I told Ted. He drove me to the abortion clinic where I had made an appointment with a counselor.

"We cannot sign off on any abortion until we discuss all your options," she said.

"I have no options."

Free From Me

We talked for a little while, and then she said, "I can't sign off on this. I can see you are not emotionally ready."

"You will sign off on this because you don't have a choice, and neither do I." I stood up and leaned over her desk. "This would destroy my family."

She shook her head. "The only way I'll agree is if you promise to get counseling when you return to school."

"Whatever I have to do, I'll do. I can't harm my family."

With the procedure done, I returned to school and told nobody. Nor did I seek out counseling as I'd promised.

What is that noise? I fought to awaken a few nights later. *I hear a baby crying.* I clutched the sheets in bunched fists. *I hear* my *baby crying.*

It was dreadful. Finally, I went to the school nurse, seeking relief.

"You'll have to see your family doctor if you want a prescription for anxiety."

I made the appointment for my next visit home.

"What's going on, Connie? Why are you depressed?"

"I'm just anxious over my schoolwork. I only need medicine to calm me down some."

The next time I saw Ted, I told him, "Sex is off the table. I can't go through that again. I just can't."

During one of his nightly calls to my dorm, Ted screamed, "You should've been in your room 10 minutes ago. You're sleeping around!"

"I am not. I was studying at the library."

"Don't you lie to me. You're nothing but a slut."

Ted was drinking more and harassing me more. I stayed with him because I believed I could do no better.

Finally, I started having sex with him again just to stop his haranguing. I got pregnant again.

"Enough's enough," I said to my friend April. "I can't do this anymore, and I can't have anything that connects me to Ted."

She drove me to Charlotte for my second abortion. A few weeks later, I returned to college for my senior year.

"Some friends I know are having a party," my friend Dana said shortly after the term began. "Will you come with me?"

"Sure."

I went and met Chas, a really nice *high school* senior. We hit it off immediately and began dating. We enjoyed a great year of fun and friendship.

"I have something to tell you," Chas said, just before our respective graduations. "I joined the Air Force."

I stared at him, dumbfounded, before his mother drew me to one side. "I think, Connie, that Chas is afraid that you are ready for the next step in life, settling down, and he just realized he's only 18."

Meeting a new guy was the last thing I wanted when I accompanied my brothers to Myrtle Beach for the high school graduation weekend.

"Connie, come here." Hale called over to me as I chatted with some friends by the beach.

Free From Me

"There's someone I want you to meet."

I walked over.

"This is Scott. Scott, my sister, Connie."

I took one look at this guy, dressed entirely in black and wearing sunglasses at night, and walked away. *That guy's got all the earmarks of a drug dealer. Mullet haircut. Gold chain necklace. Earrings. What the crap were you thinking, Hale?*

A month later, while cruising Main with my friend Linda, I heard a male voice call my name. I looked around and saw only strange faces.

The guy called my name again.

"Do you know these people?" I asked Linda. "And who is that guy calling my name?"

"That's Scotty Holt," she said. "You know him."

"No, I don't. Who the crap is Scotty Holt?"

"Yes, you do. You met him at Myrtle Beach."

I looked at him, standing next to his dad's work truck. *This is the guy I thought was a drug dealer? He looks so different without the sunglasses, black clothes and bling.*

I pulled over into the parking lot, and we began talking.

"Would you go out with me on Friday?" Scott asked.

"Sure."

Scott

I met Connie after I'd enlisted in the Air Force but before Basic Training.

Dirty Little Secrets

Our relationship began as I rebounded from my failed relationship with Cathy and Connie rebounded from Chas. Perhaps the fear of being alone was our strongest tie, but the closer I got to leaving for Basic Training, the more uncertain I became of having a committed relationship.

I pulled her aside. "This is going too fast."

"Okay."

Seriously? No fighting. She sure isn't possessive and jealous like Cathy. I like that. And she's funny and goal oriented. I like that.

I called again the next day. "Can I come over?"

The more I waffled, the less patience Connie showed. This back-and-forth endeavor occurred a few times.

"Scott, we're done."

Basic Training toned my body, and the isolation from friends and family helped me evaluate my life.

A. I'm done with the party life.

B. I'm done with partying and drugs.

C. I'm ready to settle down and have a family.

D. I'm ready to commit to Connie. I miss her humor. I want to marry that girl.

I started writing her letters. A few weeks later, I dialed her home number from the base pay phone, knowing I was only allowed one to three minutes per call.

"Connie, I'm ready to settle down, and I want a wife. Will you marry me?"

A long pause.

"Connie? I miss you. Will you marry me?"

"Okay."

The 90-second conversation ended on that promise.

Connie

"Did I just say yes?" I stared at the phone in my hand. *I didn't even realize Scott and I were still "on." He's blown hot and cold so many times. Crap, I was just done with it all.*

I loved Scott, and I felt he loved me. Neither of us wanted to be alone in life. Also, I wanted away from my dysfunctional family and wanted to start a normal family of my own. I felt Scott's family was far more stable than mine, and I knew he had big plans for his life — Air Force, college and then a business career.

Also, Scott had never yelled at me or slapped me around. A welcome relief after Ted's and my brother's abuse.

I knew Scott admired my desire to become an orthodontist. Besides being overweight in junior high, I also had crooked teeth that required braces and understood the shame associated with it. I wanted to help other kids look better, too. I'd applied to one medical school, but I hadn't received a response when Scott and I became engaged.

"Have you ever considered nursing?" Dad asked. "If you're going to marry into the military, nurses are needed, and you should always be able to find work, no matter where Scott gets stationed."

"That sounds like a good idea."

Dirty Little Secrets

I was accepted to the University of South Carolina's School of Nursing in Columbia and moved in with Scott's parents who were then living nearby. The Air Force sent Scott to Illinois. We planned a May wedding because Scott had two weeks of leave at that time.

May came, and we gathered at the church for the wedding rehearsal. As I waited for my cue to move forward, panic struck. I turned and fled to the ladies room and locked myself in a stall. My best friend, Denise, came after me.

"What's going on, Connie?"

"I don't think I can do this." I sat on the commode and doubled over, rocking back and forth.

"Do what? Marry Scott? Why not?"

"This all happened too fast. And Chas has been calling me and telling me he still loves me. I'm not sure if I'm ready for this. For Scott. For marriage in general. What if this is the wrong decision?"

"Do you love him?"

"Well, yes, but …"

"But, what?"

"A couple of weeks ago, while I was dusting furniture, Scott's mom came in the room and said she doesn't think he's ready to get married. Not even his mother thinks this is a good idea. What if I end up divorced like my own parents?"

"That's not going to happen, Connie," Denise said, "because you won't let it happen."

A couple of deep breaths later, I unlocked the stall

door and returned to the rehearsal. Scott looked unfazed. I felt a flicker of confidence. We married and honeymooned in the mountains. Then Scott returned to Illinois and I to his parents' home.

"I'll see you when you come up at Christmas," he said.

I flew to Illinois for the two-week school break, and soon after I returned to South Carolina, I learned I was pregnant. I called Scott.

"I'm a little nervous about telling my folks," I confided.

"Why?"

"They tend to judge everything I do, and Dad's always been disappointed in my decisions, anyway."

"It'll be fine."

"You'll tell your parents, right?"

"Yes, I'll take care of that."

I drove home to Newton for the weekend and told both my parents. Neither said anything negative, and I returned to Columbia filled with joy.

I finally get to keep a baby. The pain of losing the other two began to abate. *My parents are cool with it. That was a pleasant surprise. And Scott promised to tell his folks while I'm gone.*

I let myself into his parents' home and found them watching TV in the den. I refrained from bouncing into the room, but my hands trembled with excitement.

"I guess Scott told you we're having a baby."

"Yeah, but we have mixed feelings about it."

Really? I stared at his mother.

"Of course, we're excited to have our first grandchild,

but we feel you could've timed it better." I turned and stumbled to my own room, silently shutting the door.

I'll have to be very, very careful around his folks from now on. I can't deal with any more hurt and rejection.

I found a way to finish nursing school in Illinois, and five months into the pregnancy, Scott and I finally lived under the same roof. We started our "together-married" life with Scott working three jobs and playing soccer, while I finished my nursing training and took a part-time job. We were still paying off $5,000 in debt for taking out a personal loan to pay for our wedding.

We welcomed our first daughter, Hayley, just before a move to Arizona. Both events increased our debt. We both worked, and Scott spent his leisure time on the soccer field, while I spent my non-working hours taking care of our daughter.

On any typical day, Scott came home from work, passed me in the kitchen cooking dinner and took the phone out on the back porch to call his parents back in South Carolina.

Those apron strings aren't strangling you, buddy, they're strangling me. I slammed a pot on the stove.

"Why do you dislike my parents?" Scott asked when I threw plates and cutlery on the table.

"I don't dislike your parents, I dislike *you*," I fired back. "You talk to your parents for hours almost every night. You need to cut those strings and work on communicating with me instead."

What is the matter with them? My resentment toward

his parents grew. *They should tell Scott he needs to be talking with his wife, not them. Maybe they don't think I'm good enough for their precious son.*

I felt alienated, alone and starved. Starved for affirmation. Hungry for companionship. Devoid of a caring husband.

But worse, I saw Scott as a hands-off father, like mine had been.

Scott

Our second daughter, Macy, joined the family, but we continued living in two separate worlds. Connie resented the closeness I felt to my parents. I fumbled for ways to reconnect.

"Let's schedule a 'date' night. This Friday when I get off work."

"How about a family night?" Connie shot back. "You never spend time with your daughters. You're always running around doing what you want to do."

"You and I need time alone," I countered.

"Family night or nothing." She spun on her heel and left.

I withdrew into myself.

Connie nagged harder.

I'm sick of walking on eggshells. I'm sick of her attitude. Everything I do is wrong in her eyes. I can't make her happy. Our home is like a silent war zone. Four years of this hell is enough.

"You're not treating me like this anymore," I said.

Connie opened her mouth. I held up my hand to stave off the flood of angry words. "I'm done. Understood?"

Our home turned into the clash of the titans. Irrepressible Force (Connie) meets Immovable Object (me). I stopped backing down, and she refused to give in. We both dug in as the Siege of the Holts dragged on.

Connie

I felt like I didn't count, so I retaliated by lobbing a continuous tirade of complaints. "You don't spend any time with the girls." "We never see you around here." "Do you have to play soccer all the time? What about us?"

While angry words exploded like shotgun pellets from my lips, my heart flip-flopped with fear. *I can't divorce. I can't put my girls through the same pain I experienced when my parents did — and I was a lot older. I just can't do that to them.*

So we separated our lives, while existing in the same space. Two armies. Two camps. The girls and I faced off against Scott. His drinking increased as his presence decreased. I pushed every button I could think of, with zero positive results.

I became an empty shell of nothingness. Go to work. Come home. Clean house. Cook. Take care of my girls. I moved through life's minutiae like an automaton.

Scott

In mid-2005, the Air Force stationed me in South Dakota and assigned me to the worst job of my life. I drank even more as I struggled to accomplish my assigned tasks. I worked seven days a week, many weeks, trying to get caught up.

When I came home each night, I wanted only one thing, to go into my "nothing box" and zone out.

Most nights, I took my wine and dinner to the garage, popped a movie into the DVD player and thought about — nothing. I stayed in that zone until I stumbled off to bed. And I made it clear to the family that I welcomed nobody in my nothing box. Nobody.

A year later, I sat at our picnic table while keeping an eye on hamburgers sizzling on our outdoor grill.

Connie stepped outside and came over to the table. "Scott. We need help. We really need help."

I shrugged.

"You're drinking more and more. I can't watch you self-medicate with alcohol anymore."

"If you think you need help, you go ahead and get it. I don't need help. I'm fine."

Not long after that, I went to the hair salon right outside the base gates and took a seat in Lacy's chair.

"The usual?"

"Yeah."

Lacy was easy to talk to. We fell into an easy friendship, talking about general issues every time I went in for a cut.

Soon, I felt comfortable enough to share my unhappy life. "Why does Connie say such things to me?"

"Let me help you understand how a woman thinks."

Many months passed. Eventually, my comfort level with Lacy turned into an interest in her. Unbeknownst to me, she was interested, too, but since I was married, I was off limits — until I expressed my interest in her.

I can talk to this girl, I thought. *She listens, really listens to me, and seems to understand my problems. She's actually interested in me and my life. I've tried to talk to Connie for years. I'm tired of being tired. I need a change. What the heck? I'm going for it.*

In December of 2006, I went to the garage, pacing and thinking.

I'm leaving. Now. I want to be with a woman who cares about me. I stopped and frowned at the silent TV. *How can I do this without having a five-hour conversation with Connie?*

I straightened myself up, grabbed the doorknob and entered the kitchen. Connie stood in her nightgown, wiping down the counters. She looked up, surprised. Her lips parted.

"We'll have to talk about this later," I said, holding up one hand. "But not now. I just want to tell you that I'm filing for divorce."

I packed an overnight bag, grabbed my keys and drove to a local motel. When I returned the next morning, I found Connie in the bedroom, dressing for work.

"You sleep much last night?" she asked.

"No. Pretty much just sat and stared at the walls all night."

"I didn't sleep much, either." Connie started for the door. "I have to go now."

Connie

"Why are you home so early?" I asked Scott when I returned from work that night.

He slapped some papers on the counter. "I took the day off to see an attorney. We can figure out the financial split later and custody of the girls and all that stuff, but right now I need you to sign these."

I glanced over the pages.

"You want me to sign these, citing 'irreconcilable differences,' when we've never made the slightest effort to reconcile?" I laid the papers down. "That's a lie, and I won't sign them. Until we actually make an effort to fix the marriage, I'm not signing anything that says it's irreconcilable."

"I can't believe you!" Scott's hands shook in anger.

"There's a woman involved, isn't there?"

"No, there isn't."

"Has to be." *I know you so well, buddy, I know you can't stand to be alone. There's a woman.*

"You want me to sign these papers so you can just get on with your life with somebody else."

"No. There's nobody else. I just want to get on with my life in general."

Scott stayed in the house as he searched for a suitable place to live. One day, as I walked down our hallway with a load of laundry, Scott approached from the other end. He flattened himself against the wall to avoid any contact with me.

"If you're going to leave, then leave," I said. "Get the crap out of my house. I can't take any more hurt from you."

"Okay, I will." Scott bunked at a buddy's apartment until he could secure one for himself.

Although shell-shocked, I determined to keep up the appearance of a woman in control of life. I applied my makeup with the same care every morning, stayed pleasant at work, came home, cleaned my house and took care of my girls.

But I ate no food for the first four days after his announcement. *Whatever happened to Scott's promise that, even if I left him, he'd never leave me? How can he do this to our girls?*

Bitterness replaced long-held resentment.

Even though reconciliation looked impossible, Scott still called me when his job overwhelmed him.

"Why can't we work on our marriage?" I brought up the subject again after he'd unloaded all his work woes on me. "Why don't you think we can work it out?"

"Because you've never been my friend."

"What exactly is your definition of a friend?" I asked. "You still call me every time you need someone to talk to about work."

No answer.

Free From Me

I discovered something important after Scott left. I was tired of the bitterness. Tired of fighting. Tired of being emotionally distant from my daughters.

Although I'd gone to church all my life, never before had I felt a real need for God in my life.

I'd focused on me first, my marriage and my children and God second.

"Oh, God, you know what I need." I fell on my knees. "Scott's gone, so right now I need you to be my husband. I need you to be a father to my kids. Fill the gaps that Scott left, and help me get through this. Please give me the strength to get through this."

Shortly after that, I dropped my daughter off at her school and while driving home began flipping through the stations on the radio. I stopped when some lyrics grabbed me. Sanctus Real was playing "Don't Give Up." A couple of lines jumped out at me.

When did it become so easy to run from your pain?
Don't give up on love and throw it all away.

That is so us, I thought. *To the last word.*

I began including the girls in my nightly prayer time.

"Come on, Hayley, Macy." I stepped into the girls' room that night. "We need to pray together."

"What for?"

"We have to pray for Daddy because he's in a dark place right now."

Dirty Little Secrets

One night, as the girls and I held hands to pray for their daddy, I heard what I believe was God's voice: *Pray for the other woman.*

What?

But I obeyed the Holy Spirit. After I began praying for this unknown woman, God's peace saturated my being.

What is this? My marriage is trashed. I have to share my kids with this man who thinks I'm worthless and wants me out of his life. So why do I feel so calm?

I, the Eternal God, am always with you, Connie.

"Why are you holding out for someone to return who doesn't want you?" a co-worker asked. "Why don't you let him go, and find someone who wants you and will love you as you deserve to be loved?"

"God doesn't want you to be unhappy," another added.

My happiness is not God's top priority.

"How long are you going to wait?" a third asked.

"I don't know. I've left this in God's hands. He told me to hang in there and pray, and I don't think he'd have me praying for a lost cause."

A friend introduced me to an organization known as Rejoice Marriage Ministries.

They suggest telling ourselves: *I AM STANDING FOR THE HEALING OF MY MARRIAGE! I will not give up, give in, give out or give over until that healing takes place.*

As they reminded me, I *did* make a vow and exchange rings and pledge myself to Scott "for better or worse, for richer or poorer, in good times and in bad."

Free From Me

So now was not the time to "sit down, let down, slow down, calm down, fall down, look down or be down until the breakdown is torn down!"

I made their words my motto. I resolved to stand for the healing of my marriage until God brought Scott home. Not Connie. God.

As I quit focusing on my problems, I found enjoyment in new friendships, began going to a new church and attended small-group Bible studies.

I became content with my life as it *was*, not as I *wanted* it to be.

Charlotte, a nurse who lived behind me, became a good friend. When her husband, Kurt, got a job promotion, she moved to the state capital.

Not long after that, I got a frantic phone call from Kurt. "Charlotte's had a heart attack and was life-flighted to Rapid City. The doctors say there's no hope."

Another friend Laura and I drove to the hospital the next day.

"I don't know what to do," Kurt said. "How can I let Charlotte go? We have kids at home. But the doctors say I need to face reality and pull the plug."

"There is no reality except God's reality," I said. Laura and I stood on either side of Charlotte's bed and began to pray.

"God's not done with her life yet," we both said. I turned to our unconscious friend.

"Charlotte, you're going to turn 45 in March. I'm coming here with chocolate cake, and I expect you to be ready to eat it. And, furthermore, this hospital garb does nothing for you."

Charlotte eventually regained consciousness, ate the cake and moved on to rehab.

A few weeks later, I called her. "I'm coming up to rehab on Friday," I told her, "to get you ready to see your kids."

I took Charlotte down to the shower room, and we had just returned to the room when Kurt said, "Scott called."

"My Scott?"

"Yes."

"How in the world could he know where I'd be?"

"Well, the phone in your purse rang, and I wasn't about to answer it. After a little while, the room phone rang. Apparently, Scott called your house, and your daughter told him you were here."

I punched in Scott's number as I left the rehab center. "I understand you called. What's up?"

"Can you come over?"

"To your place?"

"Yes."

"Now?"

"Yes."

"Okay."

As soon as Scott opened the door, he said, "I just need you to know upfront that I didn't call you over here because I want to get back together."

Okay. Still, God's peace caressed me.

Free From Me

"I just need somebody I can talk to."
"Okay."

Scott

"I'm leaving Connie."

"I don't want to be a home-wrecker." Lacy spread her hands wide.

"Whether I'm with you or another woman doesn't matter. I'm done with Connie, regardless of what else happens. I've been thinking about leaving her for months, and now's the time. I'm getting an apartment and moving out of the house." I stood up. "You decide whether you want to be with me or not."

She decided to take a chance on me.

We had to keep the affair hidden because of Air Force regulations, adultery being grounds for dishonorable discharge. No real dates. No eating out. Never to be seen in public. The most we could do was visit each other's apartment and watch TV or movies.

Although finally away from Connie and enjoying an affair, I felt like I'd sunk into a dark hole and became even more depressed. I lived for the weekends my daughters came over because then I could get out of my apartment and do things with them.

I got deployed, then returned to South Dakota and waited for a legitimate divorce to get on with life. I thought the chance would finally come in 2008, almost two years after our split.

The judge denied the decree. She admitted that in her

15 years as a judge, she had only denied a divorce one other time. I couldn't believe Connie still wanted me back as her husband after I had repeatedly and very directly told her I didn't love her anymore and never, ever wanted to get back with her.

"Irreconcilable differences" wasn't going to be my escape from the impossible sameness.

Same circumstances. Same trap. Same despair.

"I brought a movie for us to watch," Lacy said. "My friends tell me it's really good."

We sat down and began to watch *Fireproof*, which is about a fireman who becomes so self-absorbed he almost destroys his marriage.

"We need to talk." As the final credits rolled, I looked at Lacy. "What we're doing is wrong."

Lacy actually felt the same way. "Yes, I know. We've discussed this before. We can't go anywhere or do anything except to sneak over and watch movies together."

Even though I had professed a relationship with God from a young age, I'd blatantly turned my back on him through the choices I made, including the affair.

You need to end this, I'd felt God telling me, repeatedly. *And repair your marriage.*

Each time, my response had been, "Nope. Not happening."

Fireproof became the catalyst that turned me back to

Free From Me

God. He knew my heart, how I wanted and didn't want the affair to end. *You have my attention now, God, but I'm still not going back to Connie.*

Lacy and I continued discussing our options regarding the affair. She solved the dilemma by moving to Florida.

I called my parents not long after, in despair. I was lost. I was in pain. I was alone.

"Don't you have anybody you trust that you can talk to up there?" my dad asked.

"Well, yeah, Connie. She's the only person I can trust."

"Then call her."

Connie came over as promised and remained calm, even after I told her I had no interest in getting back together. I spilled out the whole ugly two-years-of-sneaking-and-lying truth to her.

She stayed calm! Who is this woman? This isn't the Connie I know and avoid.

"I'm sorry, but I have to go," she said, hours later.

Why do I feel so much better? I wondered after she left. *I feel lighter than I have in years.*

Over the next few days, we spent hours talking, either in person or on the phone.

"Even though you're not interested in getting back together," Connie told me, "I want you to know that I forgave you a long time ago. God's had me standing for our marriage, so there's been no reason for me to wait for you to come back before I forgave you."

That night, I sat alone on my couch and faced myself in the dark. *Why am I so drawn to Connie? She's changed so much, I don't even know the new Connie. Is this for real? Would she keep being this understanding and nice if I went back?*

You need to go home, I felt God tell me.

"But what if she treats me like before? I can't take it."

I fell on my knees in front of my recliner. "I'm so tired, God," I sobbed. "I'm so done with it all."

I laid my head in the chair.

Scott, I felt God say. *You are going home. To Connie. I am going to restore everything.*

All the guilt and shame of my decisions and actions dissolved in the same peace Connie had found.

I called Connie the next day.

"I would really like to come home."

❧❧❧

Scott

We moved back south and began looking for a church home in Columbia, South Carolina.

"You girls are old enough to take part in our decision. All four of us have to be in agreement before we settle on a church."

We visited several churches but came to no unanimous agreement. Connie drove past the Vive Church often, and we checked out its Web site.

"Shall we try it?" we asked the girls.

Free From Me

We attended one Sunday, and all of us felt the same: "This is home."

Vive is a safe haven for people like me, who have sinned hard and need God's total forgiveness. Even though Connie and God forgave me, I still often struggle with the temptation to put myself first. Through Vive, I've met men I can trust who encourage me to be a better man, husband and father. I share my weaknesses with them, knowing they'll never judge me.

The greatest thing my life has taught me is to put my faith not in myself and my desires, but in God's endless, unconditional, amazing love.

Living With a Purpose
The Story of Markus
Written by Alexine Garcia

It was a cool afternoon as I rode my moped home from my friend's house. I stopped at a crossroads behind a yield sign and looked around to make sure no one was coming. On the right side, a bridge came down and curved from another road, creating a blind spot. I didn't see anyone and went on my way. Suddenly a car sped down from the bridge and hit the back of my moped. My vehicle and I tumbled onto the roof of the car before the moped was thrown 100 feet away. A firefighter found me lying lifeless 150 feet away in the opposite direction.

My body remained limp and unresponsive in a coma for the next 18 hours. When I woke up in the hospital, my family was relieved until they realized I was completely paralyzed. Their hearts sank deeper as the doctors told them I suffered amnesia. Each day, friends and family visited my bedside.

Within a couple of days, my toes and fingers began to tingle with feeling. Then my mind returned to me as I was able to recognize my visitors. Only two weeks later, I walked out of the hospital. My teachers and friends helped me recover the lost school time, and I ended up graduating from high school right on time.

"You are supposed to be dead," my mother said,

looking me straight in the eyes. Her look was solid, and her words hung heavy in the air between us. "God is not done with you. He has a purpose for your life."

☙☙☙

I was born and raised in the countryside town of Tournai, Belgium. Farmlands, green scenery and cloudy, wet weather surrounded my home. When I came to the United States on vacation, California seemed a whole new world for me. The sunny, dry weather, the beach and the palm trees and the beautiful blend of Mexican-American culture all made for a paradise-like experience. I was only there for a few weeks, but I loved it. It was so amazing that I could drive from mountains to beachside all in one car ride. I grew even fonder of this place when I met Myrna. She was a beautiful young Mexican-American girl, so full of life. We talked about our different cultures and got to know each other at the birthday party of a mutual friend. She also spoke about her faith like it was something fantastic. I spent my childhood attending a Catholic church and completed all of my holy sacraments. I knew my religion well, but it never seemed like anything great to me, much less exciting and fun. As we got to know each other better over the next few days, she urged me to dig into my own faith.

"Read your Bible, Markus. If you read it every day, I promise you will see your life change."

"You mean reading this book will change my life?"

Living With a Purpose

"Yes. It's not just any book. It's God's word. Give it a try."

The funny thing was that I did start to read it. And I actually started to like it. Then I went to a church service with her, and I was really surprised. It was far different from the wooden pews, candle lighting and rigid conservative atmosphere that I was used to. The pastor stepped up to the pulpit and actually preached about things I understood. He taught about topics that were relevant to my own life. I saw his preaching as advice I could use in my future.

"It is important to preserve your marriage," the pastor said from the pulpit. "If you are not taking the time to guard your heart, temptations will lure you away from your spouse." It surprised me to hear him speak so openly. This is something I would have never heard at a Catholic Mass back in Belgium.

When I called home to tell my brother of this Baptist church, he laughed at me. "You must be crazy. I would call Mass a lot of things, but fun is not one of them."

"No, man, you don't understand. This isn't Mass. They actually talk about things that matter in life."

But he just couldn't wrap his mind around the idea. For me, this really felt like a new step in my life. I understood the idea of confessing our sins to God because this was a big part of my Catholic faith. But now as my faith was blooming, I understood the daily act of renewing and sticking close to God. One day, I sat in church and felt my faith transforming into something brand new.

Something else happened deep inside of me as well; a deep sense of gratitude began to grow. I looked around at my life and found so much to be thankful for. I understood what it meant when they talked about a relationship with Christ. Accepting him in my life and becoming a Christian made sense. It was what I wanted.

☙☙☙

Meeting Myrna and having to head back to Belgium so quickly really had me thinking with hasty emotions. I returned home and just couldn't get her out of my mind. We began talking and sending e-mail messages, and before I really realized what was happening, we were pretty much carrying on a long-distance relationship. My emotions grew with each phone conversation. I shared my thoughts with her, and she told me about all her plans. She continued to share her faith and encourage me in my own growing faith.

I took the time to visit her about three times a year while we dated. We saw all the fun tourist attractions together, and our feelings grew stronger. But the more I cared about her, the harder her parents tried to keep her away from me.

"They are just old-fashioned."

"But you are an adult. Don't you think they should give you freedom to make your own choices?"

"It's just part of our culture. You know they love you. They are just over-protective."

Living With a Purpose

I never could take her on overnight trips because she was not allowed to be in a hotel room with me. I had to bring her home each night and felt the constant, watchful eye of her father.

I loved vacationing, but I knew I wanted more from our relationship. I was excited when my work offered me a job in 2007 that required a move to the United States. I saw this as a new step, so I accepted the offer. I lived in Columbia, South Carolina, and Myrna still lived in San Diego.

We were on opposite coasts of the country, and the reality of the distance slowly seeped in. Our relationship didn't change.

"When are you going to come visit me?"

Her long pause stirred anxiety in my heart. I could hear her fumbling on the line. "You know my parents would never allow that, Markus."

"I just don't understand. You all know I love and respect you. I don't see what the problem is. What good is living in the same country if things are always going to be long distance?"

Myrna's parents were set in their traditional ways. They believed that family should stay close. They were not willing to let their daughter move to live with someone she was not married to.

For my part, I was not ready for marriage. I wanted to live together and make sure our relationship was going to work before I made such a commitment. It only made matters worse when she never came to visit.

Dirty Little Secrets

In March of 2008, we broke up and stopped all contact with each other.

I missed her terribly. It was hard to give up on something after I thought I had met the girl of my dreams. I was forced to cut off a whole portion of my life that included very intense feelings. I came to the United States with no family and no friends, so I had little else to do besides work. Over the next few months, work became my life. The loneliness of this routine only grew more vast. It became clear that I should do something about it. Other than my job, I had little else going for me.

In June, I posted a profile on a dating Web site and began looking through the different pages of women in South Carolina. The first and only woman I met was Megan. She liked traveling and international languages. *Here is a girl who won't mind a language barrier and my funny accent,* I thought to myself. She was beautiful in all the pictures she sent. Her eyes glowed a brilliant blue, and she had shoulder-length dark-brown hair. It turned out I was the only man she met on this dating site as well.

Our e-mails progressed to phone calls. I wanted to know everything about her, and judging by all of her questions, she felt the same way about me. We had interests and goals in common, which gave us so much to talk about. Soon we were planning on meeting. Megan lived two hours away in Spartanburg. As I made the trip through the winding green roads of the South, I could hardly force myself to slow down and drive the speed limit.

Living With a Purpose

I recognized her right away when I arrived at our meeting place, a bowling alley. She was even prettier in person. I was glad we started the day with some bowling instead of a meal. I felt nervous, and the activity and loud bowling alley kept the mood light. Later that day, we drove up to Chimney Rock, North Carolina, and sat by the pier at Lake Lure and told each other even more about our lives.

"So what do you think of the Bible?" she asked.

I could hardly pay attention with those blue eyes staring at me with so much intensity. "Well, I believe it's true. I have read several portions, and I like the way it applies to every aspect of my life."

"That's awesome. Do you think you'd like to visit my church sometime?"

I wasn't sure if I'd like her church as much as the church I had visited in San Diego, but this beautiful girl really had my attention.

"Sure, that sounds nice."

The next week, her pastor was indeed just as compelling as the other Christian preacher I met. He was open about what the Bible said and how it applied to our lives.

Each weekend, I returned to visit Megan. We went to church every Sunday, and I began to realize that this weekly refreshing of my faith was another aspect of life I had been missing. Watching Megan live out her faith through kindness, volunteering and just in the simple way she lived was so encouraging.

Dirty Little Secrets

I knew this was the girl I needed to marry. Again, I felt a deep gratitude to God.

In September of 2009, we got married, and she moved to Columbia with me. Bringing our two lives together was a fun challenge at first.

I woke up at 6 a.m., read the newspaper and ate my breakfast with the light of sunrise beaming into the kitchen. I walked over to the bedroom around 8 a.m. and peeked in. Megan was still wrapped between the blankets, deep in sleep.

I'd lived alone for more than seven years now, so sharing my space with someone completely different than me proved a learning process. I was very tidy and meticulous about certain things. I liked to have my laundry clean at all times. My clothes had to be ironed and hung nicely. I never liked to see any dishes in the sink. But to Megan, these things were not important. She'd grown up in a house with a stay-at-home mom who took care of her every need.

Coming home from a long day and having to take care of all these chores that Megan let fall by the wayside began to wear on my patience. I understood that she was immersed in schoolwork, but it was a bit out of hand. She couldn't see that I needed her help in these things, and a tiny seed of resentment began to form.

My work was going extremely well. In 2012, I received a promotion to manager in charge of the Product

Living With a Purpose

Management Department. This was an excellent career move, however, it came with a downside. I began traveling domestically and internationally about three weeks out of each month.

After the first few months, Megan would greet me with open arms at the airport. "It feels like you have been gone forever," she'd say. We'd hold hands as we walked to the car.

"I'm glad to be home."

Then only a few days later she was driving me right back to the airport and hugging me goodbye. I became well acquainted with the hard airport chairs, the small cafes and long international flights. The strange all-day sluggish sleepiness of jetlag became a normal part of my life.

One evening I was finally sitting in front of the television relaxing before bed in my hotel room in China. My cell phone buzzed on the side table, and I looked down at the screen.

"Hey there, stranger," the text read. I could hardly believe my eyes. A text from Myrna.

"Hello there," I texted back.

"How have you been?" It was so strange to receive texts from her after all this time.

"Good. Actually, I am married now."

"Wow, congratulations."

I wasn't even sure what to say next. My stomach turned into a knot as I looked down at the phone. "It was nice talking to you," I texted, ending the conversation.

Dirty Little Secrets

Such a simple text conversation, yet it started a whole string of events.

☙☙☙

Back home, I peeked into our bedroom well past 11 a.m. to see Megan sleeping. She emerged from bed still in pajamas well past noon.

"Well, welcome to the day. It's half over now, you know."

She glared over at me as she poured coffee into her mug. She sat at the table across from me.

"Do you notice that all the plates you left in the sink are clean?"

"Markus, are you really going to argue with me this morning?"

"The morning is over," I said with a smirk.

"Can't we just have a nice day together?"

"Well, yes, we can. Now that I have cleaned the kitchen, done the laundry, eaten breakfast by myself, we can go have a nice day."

This was the norm for our weekend routine. We held hands and smiled, and we looked happy as we went out to the movies or shopping. As we sat in Vive Church on Sunday mornings, we looked like every other happy couple. But inside we were harboring ill feelings. I tried to keep my contempt for her to myself, but it brewed inside me every time I looked at her.

After month upon month of me traveling, we were less

Living With a Purpose

excited to see each other when I arrived home. As I spent time away from her, I became surprised at the weight she began to put on. We had always eaten healthily together. We were really living two separate lives, like roommates occasionally residing in the same home.

A large part of my life revolved around bicycling. My friend Matthew and I trained for races together. I first met him on a mountain bike trail one Sunday morning a year earlier. I helped him through a 24-hour bike ride, and we had been friends ever since. It always felt good to talk to Matthew because he shared experiences from his own life. He was 50, with three kids and a long marriage. I could see myself living that life when I was his age, so I respected and sought his advice. It was also nice to talk to him and not feel a heavy hand of judgment. I could be open, and he responded honestly.

"You know, with all this traveling you're doing, you're going to start experiencing temptations," he said one day.

I chuckled at the thought, although I felt a little thrown off by his frankness.

"I'm serious, Markus. I've been there, done that. You need to make sure you are closing all the possible doors to temptation in your marriage. People will try and pull you away from your spouse if they see the opportunity. Don't give them that chance."

❧❧❧

Again, my phone buzzed in my pocket. "How's it going on the East Coast?" Myrna texted.

"Things are great over here. How about you?"

"It could be better. School is tough. It's hard to find a good job in Cali right now. But I'm making it."

"Wow. I hope it gets better for you."

"Thanks. I have been thinking about you a lot. Glad to hear you are well."

Her text struck me hard, and again, knots began to form in my stomach.

"Actually, it's been a bit rough for me, too. I travel constantly, and I struggle with my wife. I'm happy … but it could be better."

"Well, I am sure God will help us both through our trials."

As the attraction to my wife slowly declined, my friendship with Myrna grew stronger through our text messages.

I sat at the airport in November waiting to board my flight. My heart raced as I held the vibrating phone in my hand. The screen indicated a call from Myrna. We had been texting for several months now, but this was the first time I would hear her voice since we had broken up.

"Hello?"

"Hello, Markus. It's so good to hear your voice."

"Yes, it's been a while." We carried on small talk until I had to board my plane. It was nice to hear from her. Now that we were piecing together some kind of friendship, I was less nervous about talking to her. *There is nothing wrong with a little conversation here and there,* I told myself.

Perhaps there was nothing wrong with it at that point, but the conversations became longer, and we soon started talking about our feelings. I confided in her the unhappiness I felt in my marriage. "It's so good to have a friend like you," I told her.

"You know, I feel the same," she responded.

I don't even talk to my wife like this. What is going on here? I asked myself. Matthew's warning was coming true, and I didn't want to accept it. *This is not temptation. This is a friendship. We help each other with our struggles,* I told myself.

Back home, Matthew and I relaxed on a water break after a long bike ride. I had taken our last conversation to heart and was wondering if these text messages were something to worry about. I confided in Matthew and told him about the situation.

"Well, the fact that you only talk to her when you are on your business trips is a bit concerning."

"Yeah, I guess you're right."

"You need to make sure that you are spending time with Megan. Your work is important, but time is something you can't get back. You don't want to be my age looking back on a string of regrets. Your time with Megan will keep you focused on your marriage."

He was right. But my feelings for Myrna were growing

with each trip to China. She started calling on a weekly basis.

"You're not going to believe it. I'm going to be in San Diego next week," I said to her.

"You're kidding."

"No, not at all. We are having corporate meetings in San Diego and will be there from Monday through Friday."

"Well, are you going to come see me?"

"Do you want me to?"

"Of course!"

She hadn't changed a bit from the last time I'd seen her. She greeted me with a huge hug and a customary Mexican kiss on the cheek. We walked through the mall and talked like we had never been apart. I took her to dinner that evening, and it felt almost like a date.

"If you are so unhappy with her, why do you stay with her?" She looked me in the eye, waiting for my answer. A million follow-up questions swam in those dark brown eyes.

"It's not that easy to just pack up and leave."

"But you are not happy. I could make you happy." We stared at each other silently for a moment as each of us contemplated the idea.

From that moment forward, my mind became a wreck. *God, have I made a mistake marrying Megan?* I began to question. *Could I leave Megan and marry*

Living With a Purpose

Myrna? The next week I was present at my work physically, but my mind spun with crazy ideas.

My questions turned into rationalizations. *I can divorce Megan and close that chapter in my life. She is feeling this lack of emotion for me as well, so she will understand. On top of all of that, Myrna needs me. She's struggling to make ends meet. I can be there for her.*

On the flight home, I began to put my words together. I imagined Megan sitting in front of me, and I planned what I would say to make her understand the next step in my life.

We sat down in the living room looking at each other, just as I had imagined. But putting a plan together in my mind was so much easier than sitting in front of my wife saying the words. I struggled to get the conversation started.

"I'm not even sure how to say these things to you." I looked up at her and saw the blank expression on her face. She had no idea what was about to hit her.

"Megan, listen, I have lost my feelings for you. I don't think this marriage is really working. A couple of months ago, I started talking to my ex-girlfriend, and I think I am in love with her." I watched as my wife broke into a thousand tiny pieces.

"I don't understand," she said. Tears flowed down her face. She was silent for a moment, trying to make sense of my words. "I don't know how you could do this to me."

I didn't anticipate how painful it would be. We slept in different rooms that night because she couldn't stand to be around me. Surprisingly, she woke up early the next morning and packed a bag. She turned around and looked at me from the closet with red puffy eyes.

"What are you doing?"

"I can't stay here. I need to move somewhere else."

The idea of her leaving cut deep. I felt like I was pushing a knife into my own guts because I knew I had made this mess. All of this was my own mistake.

Markus, this is your wife, you cannot let her leave your home. You love her, I thought to myself. All of the resentment, all of the lost attraction meant nothing as I watched my wife break down and cry in the closet. I felt terrible for the decision to be with Myrna. My confusion over what to do only grew more intense. *Do I really love Myrna? Is this the right choice?* I had no one to talk to because I was so ashamed and embarrassed about what I was doing.

"Lord, help me make the right choice. Give me wisdom," I prayed. I realized that even after hearing God's advice, and hearing what I should do every Sunday at church, I had not listened to any of it, and now I was stuck in this mess that I made myself.

I dialed the international code and called my family back home. My parents had always been a positive example of a good relationship. I admired their marriage of 35 years, yet here I was doing exactly the opposite. I knew they would have good advice for me, despite my feelings of guilt.

Living With a Purpose

"Marriage is not easy," my mother said. "You do need to be happy, but it would be better to work things out with your wife. There will always be crisis in marriage, but you have to work harder and save your relationship. It's not a good idea to go back to your ex."

I knew she was right, but her words were hard to accept. She passed the phone to my brother, and I told him what I was going through. He knew about the struggles I had when I was dating Myrna.

"Brother, she is an ex for a reason, and you married Megan for a reason. You should think about that."

I appreciated the honesty of my family members and the fact that they didn't judge me. They were gentle with their advice, but honest.

Megan didn't leave our home, and I went on my usual trip that week. When I came home, she was crying on the couch. She had spent the week sick with depression. I sat down in front of her and took her in my arms.

"Listen, Megan, I don't like seeing you like this. No matter what happens, I will support you financially. I will make sure you are happy." I sat there with her in my arms waiting for her to stop crying. A thought came to mind. *Have you gone mad? You want to divorce her, but you will support her and do whatever it takes to make her happy?* My thoughts and actions made no sense.

She pulled away from me and said, "Why don't you go talk to Pastor Randy?"

The thought gave me the chills. I didn't want to talk to anybody from church about what I was doing, because at the core of the situation, I knew I was wrong. What if he judges me? But I also knew I could hardly take any more of the yo-yo-like rationalizations I was making.

I sat in his office and explained the whole situation, starting from the day I met Myrna. I stiffened, prepared for him to talk down to me. I expected nothing less. I knew what I was doing was wrong.

"Let me tell you about a friend of mine who went through a similar experience," he said. "He was married with kids when his ex came back into his life. After reconnecting with her, he realized that marrying his wife was a huge mistake. He told me he was going to divorce his wife and marry his ex. I did everything I could to convince him not to. Well, my friend went through with it. He went from being a successful man at work, a happy family man at home, to a miserable drunk who is now all alone."

That's definitely not what I want, I thought to myself.

"Have you ever played poker?" Randy asked.

"Yes, a few times."

"Well, you know that if you play, betting a little bit to the left and little bit to the right, you will never win big. It's the same with your wife. If you want to win the jackpot with your wife, you have to go all in and really focus on her. Take the time to date her. Continue to get to know her. You need to cultivate your love."

"I know that you are right," I said, staring down into my lap. "But what do I do with these emotions I have for my ex? I've got my mind all wrapped up in the idea of her.

Living With a Purpose

I was set on saving her from her financial struggles and being there for her."

"God has united you with your wife. That is who you belong with. Don't worry about your ex. God will take care of her if she puts her trust in him. God will provide her with the right man. You should probably cut off communication with her, and focus on your wife."

He gave me a straight answer, and it was what I needed. I was so thankful that I came to church and talked with him. I was expecting judgment and a harsh answer, but instead, Pastor Randy counseled me and gave me advice. What a relief. Back at home, I told Megan everything he said. She sat across from me on the couch in the same place we'd been sitting a few weeks earlier when I'd broken the news. Now I watched hope instead of pain flowing into her eyes. She leaned forward, taking in every word I said.

"Well, what did you tell him?"

"I told Pastor Randy that I love my wife." I looked at her face, realizing how beautiful she was. I knew I was stupid for ever letting my guard down to temptation.

"I love you, too. I forgive you for this whole mess." Her words were like ointment soothing the wounds I'd created in our marriage.

"We need to work on things, Megan. We need to make an effort to grow our marriage, just like Randy said."

"Well, I can tell you that I need you home more. I am really tired of being alone."

"Yes, and I am tired of cleaning and taking care of this

place when I get home tired with jetlag. I need your help with that."

We continued to discuss the things we could do to make our marriage a better one. Then we joined hands and asked God for his help.

We made it clear that we loved each other, that we should work on our relationship and do all we could to save our marriage. I looked at what I was doing, and I started fixing my work schedule to be home more often. When I was home, I took all the time I could to be with her. We made the small things in life, like cooking and going on walks, into something special.

One Friday evening, I arrived home to find her in the kitchen. She looked over her shoulder at me from the sink with a smile.

"I'm so glad you're home," she said. She came over and hugged me. "Look, we're making spaghetti tonight," she said, opening a bag full of groceries. As she chopped veggies, I began browning the meat and boiling the water. Somehow, the food tasted better when we cooked it together. We sat down at the dinner table across from each other, ready to eat our meal.

"It's your turn," she said, raising an eyebrow. Blessing the meal was something different for me when I got here to the States. Seeing the way people joined hands and prayed for their food inspired me.

A large part of my faith has been thankfulness to God. So Megan and I started taking time to praise God for everything we were thankful for that day, while blessing the meal.

I took her hand in mine and prayed, "Dear Lord, thank you for providing for our every need. Thank you for this delicious meal in front of us. But more so, God, thank you for our marriage and our friendship with each other. Thank you for taking us through hard times. You have given us a purpose and a plan. We pray in the name of Jesus. Amen."

After everything that happened and the way our marriage began blossoming, church became so much richer for me. Watching God in action became part of my everyday life.

જીજીજી

Sometimes Megan's eyes are so clear and blue that I can see my own reflection. In those moments, I can envision all of our dreams taking shape. With the way we are moving forward with each other, and with God at the center of our marriage, there is no telling how he will bless us. We hope to have children and our own house one day. For now, we continue working toward those dreams a little at a time. It is so clear to us that a marriage is something we are building. It takes work, effort and sacrifice.

I was working on remodeling the bathroom one weekend, a project I knew would eat up all of my free time. It wasn't really something I looked forward to, but I knew it had to get done. I was laying out plastic and getting paintbrushes together when Megan walked in. Her hair was tied up, she was wearing sweats and rolling up her sleeves.

"I'm ready to help. What do you need me to do?"

"Really?" I said, surprised.

"Yeah. If we get this done today, maybe we can relax and hang out tomorrow. Plus, we'll always look at this place and know we did it together."

Her enthusiasm is so amazing. This is the woman I married and the one I want to stick with for the rest of my life.

I can't wait to see what we will thank God for next.

Alive Again
The Story of Rachel
Written by Karen Koczwara

"He's talking about killing himself again," I whispered into the phone.

"Rachel, he's just trying to manipulate you like he's done before. You can't let him get to you."

"You're right." But even as I said the words, I knew something wasn't right. The hair on the back of my neck stood up, and I suddenly felt nauseous. "I'll call you back."

I slipped out of the room, nerves gnawing at me. The gnawing turned to terrible dread as I found Luke's computer chair empty. *This isn't good. Oh, no, this isn't good.*

I cracked open the garage door, heart racing as I poked my head into the dimly lit room. And then, to my horror, I discovered my worst nightmare before my eyes.

&&&

I was born in Silverton, Oregon, in 1960, only 11 months behind my older brother, Chris. Another brother, Eric, arrived two years later. My mother worked as an office manager for a doctor, while my father held several positions at one time, most notably a position as a welder at the gas company. His job installing large gas lines all around Oregon often demanded long hours, and we usually only saw him on weekends. For the most part, my early years were happy and uneventful. I met my best friend, Carolyn, in kindergarten, and we instantly became inseparable. She attended a local Methodist church, while my parents took us to the Lutheran church on Sundays. My brothers and I played together often, lining up plastic Army men and Matchbox cars on our bedroom floors. Life in our small town felt easy and predictable, but it soon took a devastating turn.

I was 10 years old, enjoying that magical month when Chris and I were the same age. Chris came down with what appeared to be the flu. My mother called the doctor to the house, and he administered an injection. "Watch him, and make sure he keeps his fluids down," the doctor ordered before he left.

Several minutes later, Chris projectile vomited, and my parents panicked. They hoisted him into the car and rushed to the hospital. But it was too late. Chris died in the car. The doctors later confirmed he'd passed away of Meckels Diverticulitis, which usually is a treatable condition. At just 10 years old, he was gone, ripped from our family in an instant.

After Chris' open casket viewing, I passed out, emotionally and physically spent. My father carried me out to the car. We all reeled in our grief, unable to cope. My father grew deeply depressed, and my mother remained lost and helpless. I grieved in my own way, but my parents were too absorbed in their sadness to address my broken heart.

Alive Again

"You need to be strong for your parents. They need you to hold it together," family friends advised me when they came to visit.

I wanted to be strong, but at 10 years old, I still needed my parents to hold me up. We never went to counseling, but instead wandered around the house like glassy-eyed strangers, trying to get through each day.

My younger brother, Eric, grew troublesome. Always a hyperactive boy, his behavior worsened after Chris' death. I tiptoed around him, trying to keep up my grades and be the perfect child to avoid further chaos in our home. Eric got into trouble with the law, and when he turned 10, the court ordered him to live in a home for juvenile delinquent boys. In just two short years, I went from being the middle child, to the oldest, to the only child at home. Life felt strangely empty and confusing.

I remained a good girl, studying hard at school and bringing home good grades. Carolyn and I stuck close together, and I was grateful for her friendship. Always outgoing, I enjoyed playing sports and cheerleading. School provided a sense of normalcy and relief in the midst of my family's grief and pain. While cheerleading, I met a football player from a neighboring town. At 6 feet, 4 inches, Brett was the best-looking guy on the team, and I was not the only girl who took notice. We began dating casually.

I graduated high school in 1978. I got a job at Safeway, but the late-night shift prevented me from enjoying a social life.

"They are hiring file clerks at an insurance company in town," my friend told me.

I landed a job there and happily traded in late nights for day shifts. Brett and I began dating more seriously, and in February 1981, we married. Several weeks later, my parents divorced after 25 years of marriage. Neither had overcome their grief following my brother's death, and their relationship had never been the same since. I sadly watched a chapter of their lives end as I began a fresh chapter of my own.

Brett and I discussed starting a family sooner than later. The doctors told us it might take a while to get pregnant, but I conceived right away.

I gave birth to a beautiful little girl, Mandy, in June 1982, and 18 months later, our precious son, Ryan, entered the world. I happily embraced motherhood but remained persistent in my career goals as well. I continued working full time and began part-time college classes following Ryan's birth.

In June 1998, I graduated Magna Cum Laude with a Bachelor of Science in social and behavioral sciences. Years later, the subject of my studies would prove ironic in the midst of tragic circumstances.

I continued to work my way up the corporate ladder, juggling a family and a career. Brett, a cardboard factory employee, remained supportive in his roles as husband and father. We attended the Catholic church occasionally and went through the rituals of participation. Brett's parents, both wonderful people whom I adored, were

Alive Again

devout Catholics, and I wanted to please them. I believed in God but wasn't sure where he fit in my busy life.

Life held a steady, comfortable pace for many years. The kids grew older, and Ryan, who suffered from ADHD, struggled in school. I worried for his future and tried to convince him to go to college or obtain a technical degree.

"You have to do something with your life," I urged him.

Ryan decided the military might be a good fit. Then on that fateful September 11, I mourned with the rest of the country as the Twin Towers crumbled to the ground in a pile of dust. President Bush talked of going to war, and tension escalated between the United States and the Middle East. I cringed as I thought of my son having to go overseas and fight on the frontlines. But he remained adamant about his decision.

I moved up to regional director of operations in my company. In 2002, the corporate office offered me a temporary position in Illinois. Brett and I discussed it, and he agreed it was a great opportunity for my career. Both of us had lived in Oregon our entire lives, however, and the idea of starting over fresh intimidated me a bit. I accepted the yearlong position as corporate billing director, intending to clean up the division and streamline operations in Illinois.

Though exciting, the job proved detrimental to my marriage. Brett grew lonely with me gone. By now, the children had grown up and moved out of the house, and when I came back to Oregon on the weekends, things felt strained at home. When the company offered me full-time employment in Illinois, I accepted the position. But I lost my marriage at the expense of my promotion. Brett and I divorced in 2004, going our separate ways. I regretted my decision later, wishing I'd tried harder to make our relationship work. We remained good friends, even as we said goodbye to a life we'd built together.

Ryan joined the military, and to my chagrin, he headed off to a tour in Iraq. I said many prayers for him, pleading with God to bring him home safely. I had not prayed much in my life but figured there couldn't be a better time to start than now.

Ryan called frequently, and I learned he'd lost half his platoon in the first six weeks of deployment. My stomach lurched at the idea of losing my precious son.

Often, while walking through the airport on business trips, I caught snippets of war footage on CNN. I grew sickened as the newscasters discussed the growing death toll.

Please, God, not my son. Please let him survive and make it home safely.

After Ryan returned from his first trip to Iraq, he called me and began to discuss spiritual matters. "Mom, what do you think of the Bible?" he asked. "How much have you read?"

"I've read parts," I replied casually. "Why?"

"I read the whole Bible twice when I was in Iraq."

"Really?" I was impressed. "Well, where do you stand on all of it? Are you a Christian now?"

"I'm gonna play it safe and say yes, I am," Ryan replied. "But I've still got some valid questions. Like, why is Jesus always portrayed as this handsome white guy? He was from the Middle East, where I've just been. You know that, right?"

I laughed. "Good point." I hung up, mulling over our conversation. If God had brought my son home safely from Iraq, perhaps the least I could do in return was read my Bible.

Ryan returned to Iraq again. I sent up more prayers, my stomach tightening every time I walked past those TVs at the airport and caught footage of the war. I'd never paid much attention to the news, but now, my son was one of those soldiers fighting on the frontlines for our country. Ryan continued to call as often as he could, and though he remained vague with his stories, he occasionally shared one with me.

"Me and these three guys were patrolling a rooftop, walking in a straight line as we looked for insurgents below. Suddenly, a sniper shot one of my guys in the head, and he fell. Me and the other guy had to drag him to safety. It scared me so bad, Mom. It could have just as easily been me."

My heart raced as I fought for words. "Ryan, you have to lean on your faith in God. You have to stay strong," I reminded him, my eyes filling with tears.

"I will, Mom. I definitely will," he assured me.

While I remained focused on my job, I decided it might be a good idea to date. I had never really dated, as

Dirty Little Secrets

Brett had been my first and only serious love. I logged onto the popular dating site, match.com, and began exploring my options. NFL football stars, successful businessmen, fine art connoisseurs and bikers were among the eclectic group of guys I dated during the next year. I enjoyed meeting new people and determining what was important for me in a partner. Now in my 40s, my priorities had shifted a bit, and I wanted to make sure that, if I decided to marry again, I chose well.

One day, I landed on an especially intriguing profile. A guy named Luke seemed to possess every quality I was looking for. Though he lived in Chicago, nearly two hours from my home in Wilmington, he happily agreed to come my way for dinner at TGI Friday's.

The night of our date, an unexpected blizzard ripped through town, blanketing the streets with six inches of snow. My friend's SUV was to be delivered to my house, and I had to stay and wait for it. I knew my little two-seater Mercedes convertible would not hold up well in the snow. I called Luke to let him know my predicament.

"Do you mind coming over?" I asked.

"Of course. No problem," he agreed.

Luke showed up at my door, well-dressed and just as pleasant as he looked in his pictures. Though not strikingly handsome like Brett, he was attractive, and I immediately felt at ease in his presence. While we waited for the SUV to arrive, he shoveled my driveway and sidewalks. I was impressed. *What sort of guy does this? Is he dropped straight from heaven?*

Alive Again

"You look like you're freezing," Luke said. "Why don't you let me rub your feet inside?"

I didn't object. We stepped inside, and he gave me an impressive foot massage. We then headed to dinner, where we talked for hours and wound up closing down the place. Luke said that he was divorced with a son Ryan's age and two young boys. An electrical engineer, he also had a patent on something related to electrical lighting and received a hefty sum for his product every month. He also said that he volunteered at his church, which greatly pleased me, as I wanted a guy with a strong faith in God. I shared my story as well, and he listened intently, seeming genuinely interested. By the end of the evening, I was smitten. *Wow, this guy is almost too good to be true. He's smart, attentive, kind, educated and successful. I can't remember the last time I clicked with someone like this.*

Luke and I grew serious quickly. Whatever need I had, he immediately met. If I casually mentioned something I liked, he made sure to bring that exact item the next time we met up. He treated me like a queen, and I relished the attention. Back massages became a regular treat. We went to Dairy Queen every night, grabbed an ice cream cone and sat in the parking lot, talking for hours like two teenagers. We prayed together, and I respected his faith in God.

He also introduced me to his boys, who spent every other weekend with him, and I fell in love with them, too. I felt like I was walking on the clouds, my feet lighter than air when we were together. *I think this is the man for me,* I decided in my heart. *I can see myself spending forever with him.*

One day, Luke confided something important: "I just want you to know that I'm bipolar."

I nodded, absorbing the news. "Okay. Well, do you take your medication?"

"Oh, yes, of course," he assured me.

I nodded again. "Well, that's good." I knew a bit about bipolar disorder from my college studies and knew that if bipolar patients faithfully took their meds, they could live a normal, functioning life. I didn't dwell on his condition, as it didn't seem like a big deal. *Guys like Luke only come around once in a great while. I know I've found a good one.*

My friend Kelly, who rented my finished basement, met Luke and was impressed by him. "He seems really wonderful," she gushed. "I'm so happy you guys found each other."

After a year of dating, Luke showed signs of instability. He grew very controlling as well. If I flew out to visit my daughter, he called up to 25 times a day. If another man glanced at me, he insisted I was having an affair. My friends took notice of this behavior, but I brushed it off.

"Luke is bipolar, but he takes his meds," I told them. "He's got his condition under control."

Luke more than made up for his erratic episodes by treating me like a princess the rest of the time. He whisked me off to Jamaica, and we had the time of our lives. He complimented me daily and satisfied my every need. I looked past his disorder and convinced myself I'd found rare gold in my relationship with him.

When Luke proposed, I happily accepted. We discussed wedding plans, and I decided to mortgage my house to pay for our wedding. I'd always loved Maui, and Brett and I had taken the kids there several times when they were young. It seemed like the perfect romantic place to recite our vows. I made arrangements, securing an official Hawaiian minister to perform the ceremony in February 2007. As the big day neared, I grew giddy with excitement, happy to marry my best friend in paradise.

Days before the wedding, Luke's 7-year-old son came up to me and said in a small voice, "Mommy said it's too early for you to get married."

His mother is still probably struggling with the divorce. I smiled at the boy. "Don't worry, it's okay," I told him. "Your daddy and I love each other."

At last, the time arrived. We flew out to Maui, and Luke's oldest son and my kids arrived shortly after. The island was every bit as stunning as I remembered. The warm, salty air kissed my cheeks as I stuck my bare feet in the sand, and I reminded myself once again of my amazing good fortune. But trouble soon brewed in paradise. Luke's two younger boys didn't show up. I panicked momentarily, as the youngest one was to be our ring bearer. I assumed their mother found it too difficult to let them go, and I understood her decision. Little did I know, she had other reasons for not showing her support.

Four days before the wedding, Luke suffered a major

bipolar episode and became extremely agitated. He stormed around, saying strange things that made no sense. I froze, not sure how to handle his erratic behavior. My close friends and family who'd flown in for the ceremony approached me with concern.

"Are you sure you want to go through with this?" they asked.

I took a deep breath, thinking of the whopping $30,000 I'd spent on wedding expenses. *I have to go through with it. I'm sure it will all be fine. I know Luke's bipolar, but as long as he's on his meds, it shouldn't be a problem at all.*

We visited a notary, where we signed the marriage certificate and swore before the state that we freely and legally chose to commit ourselves to marriage. At the actual ceremony, both sets of my parents were present. If I had watched the videographer's footage of that moment, I would have noticed the vacant look in Luke's eyes. It was as if he was absent, a shell of a person reciting his vows. Something was not quite right.

Shortly after we wed, I learned the startling truth. Luke was still married to his wife, Carrie. Though they'd begun divorce proceedings, their marriage was not yet legally dissolved. I gulped hard, remembering his agitation just days before the wedding, as well as his son's remark. It all made sense now. *How could he have been dishonest like this?*

I prayed fervently, begging God for wisdom. Luke was wonderful in so many ways, unlike any guy I'd ever met.

Alive Again

His boys had already accepted me as their stepmother, and I'd grown especially fond of them. But could I stay married to a man who'd so blatantly lied to me?

"Luke, I don't know if I can do this," I told my new husband. "You were dishonest and lied to me about a pretty major thing. I think it might be best if we go our separate ways." It stung to say the words aloud. I thought of our first date, how he'd rubbed my frozen feet until they thawed. I remembered our long conversations in the Dairy Queen parking lot, how we'd talked about everything under the sun. *This guy is too good to be true,* I'd thought to myself. And now I was afraid he really was.

"No! We can work things out! Please, Rachel! Don't leave! I'll kill myself if you do!" Luke begged, his eyes desperate and pleading. "My divorce from Carrie is finalized, with the exception of our property settlement. I assure you I've moved on. There are no more secrets."

I sucked in my breath. "Okay, we'll work it out," I said at last. I wanted to believe him, wanted to hope for our happily ever after. But something deep in my gut held me back, and I began distancing myself in our relationship.

I sought out a Christian therapist, who helped me work through my thoughts on divorcing Luke. "He's such a great guy, so fun to be around, so attentive, so smart," I told the therapist. "But I'm just not sure if I can trust him anymore."

I came home one day to find our dog running wild in the tiled area of the house. "What are you doing loose?" I said to the pup, suddenly sensing something was wrong. I walked toward my bedroom and heard music coming from the other side of the door. When I jiggled the knob, I found the door locked. *Okay, this is weird. What's going on?* I stuck a knife in the keyhole and pushed the door open. But I was not prepared for what came next.

Luke was lying in the master bathroom tub in a pool of sticky blood. Horror gripped me as I stood frozen to the tile floor, staring at a man I no longer recognized. Luke had sliced his wrists and elbows several times. When I stepped forward, he slit his throat in front of me.

"Leave me the f*** alone so I can finish what I started," he muttered, gripping the blood-covered knife in his hand. His eyes then rolled back into his head, and he went unconscious.

I grew weak, my pulse racing as the adrenaline pumped through my veins. I was a good girl from a decent home. I was not prepared for things like this. Yet I'd just been thrust into a horror movie, and I hadn't a clue what to do. Glancing down, I noticed several 8x10 photos of a trip we'd taken to Jamaica, scattered all over the bathroom floor, covered in blood. My stomach lurched, and I struggled to keep from collapsing. *No, no, no. This is not happening to me. Someone wake me up from this nightmare, please!*

I stumbled to the phone and dialed 911 with shaking fingers. "My husband has just tried to kill himself!" I blurted. "I need help now!"

The next few hours were a blur as social workers, police and paramedics arrived on the scene. They

Alive Again

determined that Luke was still alive but informed me he'd be placed in a mental institution after he healed. The social worker insisted I leave the state for my protection and escorted me to a plane headed to Minnesota. Like a robot, I boarded the plane, still trying to process the horrific events in my mind. *I must be living someone else's life right now. Surely, this is a bad dream.* My girlfriend Sarah took me in and watched over me for the next three months, something I will be forever grateful for.

"You know, this man is obsessed with you," the police told me before they left the scene. "It's just a matter of time before he tries to kill you, too."

Could they really be right? I wondered as the plane lifted off the ground. *Luke is troubled, for sure, but I can't imagine him ever trying to harm me. He loves me!*

Luke stabilized and convinced the doctors he was okay and ready to be released. They let him go after one month, rather than the three months he was slated to stay. He contacted me again and insisted he was doing much better, that he'd just had one of his episodes.

"I'm back on my meds now," he said. "I'm fine, really."

"Luke, I don't know if I can do this," I told him. "I really think it might be best if we ended our marriage."

"No!" Luke cried. "I can't bear the thought of losing you! Please, don't say things like that!"

I felt trapped, confused and uncertain. A small voice told me to go with my gut, to leave him for good. But another voice drowned that one out, encouraging me to give him one more chance. Though my children pleaded with me to bid him goodbye, I let him move back in with me, and we tried to resume life together. Things felt strained, however, and I tossed and turned at night, replaying the horror of seeing him lying in a pool of blood in the bathtub. What sort of guy does that? And would he really try to kill me?

One night, terrified I might leave him, Luke took three bottles of pills. He went unconscious, and I frantically dialed 911. The doctors hospitalized him once again until he could stabilize. The same police officers showed up and this time looked me squarely in the eyes and said, "You must leave this man; he *will* kill you."

In October 2007, I learned my mother was terminally ill. The news crushed me. She had been diagnosed with stage four ovarian cancer 25 years before, and the doctors had given her only three months to live. But she was determined to see my children grow up, and so she hung on. She'd remarried a wonderful man after divorcing my father, and they'd lived an active life. Somehow, I convinced myself my mother was invincible, immortal even. She was the rock, and I couldn't imagine getting by without her. I quit my job and moved to Oregon to be with her in her last days. The move gave me a chance to clear my head and get away from Luke, as well as spend precious time with her.

Being back in Oregon brought welcome relief. As difficult as it was to see my mother in pain, I cherished my time with her, far away from the madness of my own life. Now away from Luke, I was able to think things through

Alive Again

clearly. *I need to file for divorce once and for all. I can't keep going on this way. This guy is a ticking time bomb. He is not the man I thought he was.*

I filed for divorce, and in April 2008, my mother passed away. Grief overwhelmed me. Losing my brother had been terrible, but losing my mother was quite different. It was impossible to imagine not being able to call her on a whim, not being able to share another laugh or a good cry. My life was unraveling quickly, and I didn't know how to put the pieces back together again.

In August, Luke called me from the garage of our home. "I am going to kill myself by carbon monoxide poisoning," he said, his voice despondent.

"No, Luke, don't do that," I begged. "It's all going to be okay." My heart thudded as I hung up the phone. *Here we go again.*

I called my neighbor, who had a key to my home. "I need you to call 911 and let the responders in," I told her. "Luke is suicidal again."

The responders arrived and placed Luke in a mental ward of the hospital for two weeks. Once again, he convinced the doctors he was well enough to leave. In November, he called again, this time to tell me he wanted to go away and die alone. I kept him on the phone and tried to talk him down from his suicidal ledge, but he remained distraught.

We communicated for the next several months via Skype, and my stomach knotted with constant worry. I saw the desperation in his eyes as we talked through the computer screen, and I knew he was in bad shape. He began to drink heavily and soon revealed that he was a recovering drug addict and alcoholic. I reeled at yet another bombshell. *This guy never drank or did drugs around me. He really fooled me. I thought he was the perfect Christian gentleman. Boy, was I wrong.*

The following April, Luke flew out to Oregon to try to reconcile with me. We spent time at the serene Oregon coast, taking in the fresh, salty air and watching the waves roll over the rocky shore. Though we enjoyed a few good moments, he quickly succumbed to depression again. I gently told him that though I cared about him, I did not think we could be together again. He flew back to Illinois and called me multiple times a day. My pulse quickened every time the telephone rang, not knowing what to expect when I picked it up. He continued to talk of death, and I tried to brush it off. *He's manipulating you, Rachel. Just remember, he's tried this trick before. He's very good at what he does, but you can't fall prey to his threats again. You can't fix this guy.*

As the talks of suicide continued, however, I grew worried about him living in my house alone in Illinois. In December 2009, I flew back for the weekend, determined to find him another place to live. I went to dinner with a Christian girlfriend, and she prayed with me that night, asking God to help Luke obtain peace and understand why I needed to remove him from my life.

"Thank you for praying. You have no idea how much that means to me," I told her. Though I had not gone to church consistently in my life, I believed in God, and I strongly believed in the power of prayer. I had prayed fervently for God to protect my son while overseas in Iraq, and he had brought him home safely. I knew God would carry me through this situation, as excruciating as it felt right now.

On December 12, I arrived home after dinner to find Luke sitting at the computer. He had written a suicide note, leaving all of his possessions to me. I panicked, slipped into the bedroom and phoned his sister to express my concerns.

"He's talking about suicide again," I whispered. "I really don't know whether to take him seriously or not."

"It's just his way of trying to manipulate you, remember, Rachel?" she said. "Just be strong, and don't let him get to you. He's done this before."

But as we continued talking, I got an eerie feeling, and the hair on the back of my neck stood up. "I'll call you right back," I whispered. I hung up and walked back into the computer room. But Luke was not there. I froze, knowing something was very, very wrong. This was not like the other times. I had a very bad feeling.

When my search around the house proved futile, I stepped out into the garage. There, to my horror, I discovered Luke had hung himself. *Nooooo!* I raced toward him, thinking perhaps I could lift him up and save him. But he was too heavy, and his body did not budge. Sickened, I ran back into the house and called his sister back.

"He did it," I cried, my voice so shrill I hardly recognized it. "He hung himself!"

"Oh, Rachel! Oh, my gosh. I'm on my way. Did you call 911?"

"No." I'd been too horrified to consider calling for help. I hung up and dialed 911, my words tumbling out one on top of the other. My heart thumped so fiercely in my chest I feared it might burst. *This is a nightmare. This can't be happening to me. This sort of stuff happens on crime shows on TV, not to middle-aged women from a decent home. Oh, God, help me!*

Ten police cars and fire trucks showed up at my home, their sirens blaring. The police stepped inside and spoke to me. Their words sounded foreign and muffled to my ears. "We know you didn't do this. There is no way you have the strength to carry this out," they said.

I froze. *Wait. What? They think I killed him?* My head spun. *Surely, they know this is a suicide!*

The next few minutes were a blur, as the police confiscated computers, cell phones and the suicide note. I stood to the side, watching my once-cozy home ransacked and turned into a crime scene. I went weak. And then the reality hit me. *Luke is dead. After threatening to take his life so many times, he finally went through with it. He's never coming back again.*

The days following Luke's death were nothing short of a nightmare. Luke's oldest son and my son came to my house to help me pack all of Luke's belongings and clean the house. As I sorted through them, I felt sick. *Here is a man I thought I knew but didn't really know at all. I studied social and behavioral sciences in school. How did I not see the signs? Even when friends tried to warn me, I didn't listen to them. But they were all right. Luke was one troubled man.* In cleaning out his documents, I found lie after lie in black and white. There was far more I didn't know about this man than I actually ever knew.

I walked around in a fog, unable to sort my thoughts clearly. When I closed my eyes, the only thing I saw was Luke's face as he hung in my garage. It haunted me day and night. *It's not how it looks in the crime movies,* I realized. *It is much, much worse.* I shuddered, trying to get the gruesome image out of my mind, but it remained etched there, like a stain I couldn't remove.

I felt as if I was literally crawling out of my skin. I couldn't eat. I couldn't sleep. I simply existed, now a shell of a person, haunted by the nightmare that had just ensued in my home. It was the worst feeling I'd ever experienced in my entire life.

I returned to Oregon, but sleep still eluded me. When I closed my eyes, all I saw was Luke's face at his death. My best childhood friend, Carolyn, called to check up on me.

"I don't want you alone, Rachel," she said. "You can stay at my house, or I'm coming over there, but you are not staying alone."

I was grateful for her comforting presence. Having known me since kindergarten, she knew when I was doing well and when I was not. We clung together, trying to make sense of a senseless tragedy.

Carolyn took me to church with her, and I enjoyed it very much. With contemporary music and sermons I could relate to, it reminded me of a large church Luke and I had attended together in Illinois. I let the music sink in, and it comforted me in my confusion and grief. The pastor's messages soothed my hurting heart as well. I'd cried out to God for help many times over the years, but I'd never felt especially close to him. But now, something shifted in my spirit. I wanted a meaningful relationship with God, something deeper, something real. I desperately needed him and knew he was the only one who could provide the peace I so desperately craved.

"God, what are you trying to tell me? I'm listening to you!" I cried out.

Carolyn suggested I visit her nurse practitioner, and I agreed to go. The woman specialized in Post Traumatic Stress Disorder and diagnosed me with a severe form of it. I realized I'd suffered from PTSD after watching my mother die as well, but I had just chalked it up to the typical grieving process and never addressed it. Now, I knew I needed help, and I was grateful for answers. The therapist prescribed depression medication to help me cope and sleep medication to help me rest. She also read me Bible verses to comfort me through my wave of emotions. Hope was on the horizon at last.

Two weeks after Christmas, I met a guy named Mike. We became friends, and I enjoyed his company immensely. On the surface, we appeared very different. He was an outdoorsy guy who loved hunting and fishing. I was a poised businesswoman who preferred nice dinners and city living. But as we swapped stories, I realized how much we had in common.

He'd been married to a woman who was still married, and the dishonesty and betrayal had come as a shock. He also suffered from PTSD after a fiery explosion at work, and he understood my trauma and pain. Though I wasn't looking to date so soon after Luke's death, I truly believed Mike was sent from God to help me get through the most difficult point in my life.

Luke was cremated and had always said he'd want to have his ashes scattered on a beach somewhere, so I did just that. Mike and his daughter went with me to a secluded little Oregon beach, and we said a prayer. Just as we tossed the ashes into the ocean, a large wave rushed up, and I fell into the water. Drenched and shivering, I stood up, not sure whether to laugh or cry. Mike rushed to the store and returned with a pair of shoes and sweatpants to warm me up. His thoughtful gesture spoke volumes. *This guy is a keeper,* I decided.

Mike and Carolyn became my two rocks, helping me navigate the trenches day by day. But God became my ultimate source of strength, as I learned to rely on him for everything. It had taken me hitting the bottom to realize how much I truly needed God. Though Mike and Carolyn provided tangible comfort, God provided supernatural comfort. I truly fell in love with him for the first time in my life, and slowly, peace and joy seeped back into my heart.

Dirty Little Secrets

Three months after Mike and I began dating, I received a job offer from a company in South Carolina. I told Mike about it, expecting him to be hesitant. But instead, he said enthusiastically, "Let's go!"

I accepted the job, and Mike and I moved to South Carolina to begin a new chapter of our lives. I was now sleeping through the night and coping much better on my medication. In many ways, my rollercoaster relationship with Luke felt like another lifetime. I was happy to move on and put the past behind me. But just as I thought that might happen, a trigger sent me into a tailspin.

While driving through my new town one day, I flipped on the radio and heard an ad for a business owned by someone with the same name as my late husband. I froze in my seat, the name sinking in like a poison. *No! That's just plain cruel! Why?*

From that moment on, everywhere I went, I heard his name. It seemed I could not go anywhere without hearing or seeing it — billboards, grocery stores, radio stations. Learning that the owner of the business was a well-respected, older gentleman in town did not help a bit. He still bore the name of my late, mentally ill husband who had caused me years of grief. I burst into tears every time I heard it, unable to stop crying. *Make it stop! Make it all go away! I never want to hear that name again as long as I live!*

Searching for closure, I called Luke's ex-wife, Carrie. I pressed her for answers, wanting to know all about his past. Was everything he told me true, or had it all been a lie? Carrie confirmed what I'd already thought — most of it was a lie.

"I know you didn't know," Carrie said.

"Why didn't you tell me? Why didn't you warn me to stay away from him?" I asked.

"You wouldn't have listened," she said with a sigh.

"You're right," I admitted.

"Rachel, he told me if he couldn't have you, no one would. He was going to kill you."

Whoa! My heart jumped in my chest at her words. "Really?" Somehow, I wasn't surprised. The police had said this as well, reminding me I was very lucky to be alive. *Thank you, God, for sparing my life! Thank you for watching out for me. My story could have had a very different ending.*

Just as I settled into my new job, I endured another blow. One day, while hanging out on my back deck, my new puppy grabbed something and ran off with it. I jumped up, flew off the deck against the neighbor's fence and completely blacked out. The doctors confirmed that my sleep medication had interacted poorly with my low blood pressure, which caused me to black out. I broke my pinkie finger on my left hand, but that was the least of my problems. A series of medical issues followed, including peripheral neuropathy, a terrible burning sensation that felt as if a million bees were buzzing inside my skin. I also suffered a back injury, and my feet went completely numb. Though I was in bad shape, Mike remained by my side the entire time, and I was so grateful for his support. Without him, and my strengthened relationship with God, I would have fallen into depression again.

Mike and I married in 2011. We found Vive Church the following year after we moved to South Carolina. The moment we walked in the doors, we glanced at each other and said at the same time, "This place feels like home." Though not as large as some of the churches I'd attended in the past, I enjoyed the smaller intimate atmosphere. Several people stood at the door to greet us with warm smiles. We sat three rows behind the pastor and listened to him speak. The music was contemporary and the people especially friendly. By the time we left, I knew we'd found a place to belong.

Mike and I plugged into a small group through Vive, and I looked forward to going each week. *These are real people, just like me, with struggles and triumphs of their own. It feels great to connect and be loved.*

On January 12, 2014, I was baptized at Vive Church, sharing my faith in God in front of the whole church as the pastor dunked me under water in a hot tub the church had brought in for the special occasion. I had been baptized as a baby and had grown up attending the Lutheran church, but it wasn't until the past few years that I'd made a true commitment to God. I now understood what it meant to have a relationship with him. It meant I had someone to lean on when troubles came my way. It meant knowing he'd never leave my side. It meant talking to him when I felt alone, afraid or uncertain. It meant sharing my joy with him as well. God's love was unfailing, and he would never disappoint. I had treaded many troubled waters, but God had been my refuge, watching over me, keeping me from harm in the midst of danger and pulling me safely to shore. I had a Savior who had forgiven me, and because I'd put my trust in him, I truly believed I would spend eternity with him in heaven someday. Someday all my earthly pain, both physical and emotional, would fade away in his presence. What a wonderful feeling!

❧❧❧

"Oh, he's just precious!" I gushed, holding my new grandson in my arms. "Look at those little tiny feet and hands!"

I'd come out to Los Angeles to visit my daughter, who'd just given birth to a beautiful little boy. Between Mike's children and mine, we now had nine grandchildren. I felt so blessed to be both a mother and a grandmother and even more blessed to have a chance to share this special moment with my daughter.

Though I still struggle with back problems and neuropathy, I feel hopeful that I'm on the path to healing. My daughter's husband, who sells back equipment, connected me with one of the best back surgeons in the Los Angeles area, and I look forward to seeing if he can relieve me of my pain. But while I'm enjoying my visit, I miss attending Vive Church. It has become a second home for me, and I am so grateful I've found such a wonderful place to belong. My faith is stronger than ever now because of the great teaching and encouragement I've received since attending there.

As I reflect upon the past few years, one of my favorite Christian songs, "That's What Faith Can Do," by Kutless, often comes to mind:

> *And I've seen miracles just happen,*
> *Silent prayers get answered,*
> *Broken hearts become brand new,*
> *That's what faith can do.*

The chorus of this song seems to sum up my life so well. My journey with Luke often felt like a nightmare, one in which I'd become trapped and couldn't seem to escape. I felt as if the sky was falling, as if the ceiling of my life might cave in at any moment and leave me in a pile of rubble beneath. My heart was broken, both for Luke, a victim of mental illness, and for myself. I thought I'd found the perfect man, but instead, I discovered a stranger I never really knew. I struggled for answers, wondering how I'd ever heal and move on from the distress. But at my lowest point, God brought me hope. He met me in the darkness, provided me with supportive friends and even brought me a wonderful, supportive husband in Mike. As the song says, my broken heart has become brand new. Because of my faith in God, I have found healing, and I thank him every day for pulling me out of the pit.

I am alive again.

The Answer
The Story of Elisha
Written by Alexine Garcia

The high-pitch wail of the alarm warning of incoming mortar rockets became a part of the daily routine on our outpost in Iraq. Once we heard the sound, we had about five seconds to find cover in the bunkers. Patrols, bombs and incoming fire were just another part of life now.

We patrolled in the village one afternoon when the explosives team located a possible bomb. We used our Humvees and created a perimeter around the area. All of us watched our sectors for incoming rounds or suspicious activity. Our senses were hyper-vigilant as we quietly kept watch.

A young man zipped from around a corner right in my line of fire. He held a grenade launcher on his shoulder and shot toward our truck.

Within seconds, the loud flaming rocket whizzed by the driver's side window, missing us by inches. A surge of adrenaline and relief coursed through my veins. We had already seen more than 10 of our soldiers die. The constant question fired through my mind: *When will it be my day?*

༺༺༺

Dirty Little Secrets

When I was a kid, I'd watch my dad stagger into the house and knew he was drunk. He drank with my uncles for days on end until their money was gone.

My mom, on the other hand, would drag us to church. I always wondered why it was so important to her. The routine of walking to the chapel three times a week felt more like an obligation to me. I was still in elementary school and didn't see the reason.

Yet somehow, church changed our family for the better. When my mom started taking us to this church up the street, she seemed lighter, like some burden was lifted. She was happier, and the next thing we knew she invited everyone over to announce something special. One day, she pulled my brothers and me close, her face beaming with excitement.

"Your father is different now. He's not going to drink anymore, because he is *born again*."

I didn't get it. It had something to do with church, and that was all nice. I was reluctant to believe that anything could tear my dad away from his beer, but it was true. We watched day after day as he sobered up and came home right after work. He had always been a loving father, but now he was there for us. His brothers and other drinking buddies stopped coming around trying to entice him to go out when they realized his seriousness.

I guess he saw poor choices coming with my brothers and me, because he sat us down and lectured us.

"I got in a horrible car accident because I insisted on driving drunk. My alcoholism brought nothing good to my life or our family. I'll tell you right now, sons, nothing good comes from being out late partying."

At first, I took these chats seriously. Witnessing him emerge from that lifestyle was even more evidence that he was right. But the influence of my friends was stronger. I wanted to be accepted at school. I wanted to be one of the cool guys, and I wanted it more than I wanted to please my dad. I started drinking a beer or two with my friends in middle school. Once in high school, house parties became the regular weekend event.

Beer and bottles of liquor were in abundance one clear evening with a sky full of stars. Everyone was laughing and having a good time. Some friends and I stood around in a circle in the backyard drinking our beers. I didn't realize someone lit a joint until the guy next to me took a puff. This was it. I couldn't say no or I'd look like a fool. I wasn't even sure how to smoke this. But if I took a hit and passed it on, I would fit in. It didn't matter if I was the youngest, at 15, it didn't matter my size, how many friends I had. With this decision I'd cross a threshold into coolness, even more so, into manhood. My eyes stayed glued to the joint as it passed right to me.

"Take a hit, man," my friend said, holding the joint between his middle finger and thumb.

I took the joint and inhaled a few puffs. Thick white clouds flowed from my mouth. I didn't feel any fantastic high that first time, but it sure felt nice to be one of the cool kids.

The next few years passed in a blur of drunken weekend nights. All that mattered to me was partying, fitting in with my friends and having fun. When my grades started to slip, it didn't really matter to me, but it sure mattered to my parents.

"What are you going to do with your life?" my dad asked. He always had this same question at the tip of his tongue. Why couldn't he just back off? The week before, he'd stumbled across my stash, and his nagging became more intense than usual.

"Listen, Dad, I'm just not that into school."

"Son, all you seem to care about are those shady friends of yours. Your mother and I want you to make something of yourself."

"I just want to get my GED and graduate."

Frustration lined his face as his jaw clenched. "How is that going to get you anywhere?"

"I'll take the special courses and get my GED in a few months. Otherwise it could be two years before I finish." Already 17, I wasn't even going to graduate with my own class at this rate. I didn't feel like dealing with that embarrassment.

"You go ahead and get in that program, but I'm telling you right now, you're not going to drop out of that, too."

Within a few months, I earned my high school diploma and met a whole new group of friends from the college campus. These guys didn't mess around with the small stuff, like weed and alcohol. They introduced me to coke, speed and anything else I liked.

The Answer

Of course, completing high school didn't stop my dad from nagging. "You better believe you're not going to sit around the house all day. You're 18 now. You need to get out and find a job if you want to live under this roof."

Hanging out with my friends always relieved my stress, and this was no exception. "He never stops complaining, man. It's like I have no peace," I griped to Jimmy. We sat in his garage with our feet up, drinking a few beers.

"That's what parents do best. Mine left me alone after I joined the Guard."

"That's that Army stuff you do once a month, right?"

"Yeah, it's so easy. I literally just skate by. You should look into it."

I spoke with a recruiter a few weeks later and really liked what he had to say. I just had to show up to an Army National Guard center one weekend a month for some Army training. They offered a couple hundred dollars a month, money for college and all kinds of benefits. Better yet, I'd actually be in the Army, and my dad might stop his complaining about my life.

Truck driving was also something that appealed to me. One year, Charles, a friend from my parents' church, took me on the road with him to Colorado. It was cool being paid to drive. There wasn't much work to this job, and the pay was good. So when truck driving became available in the National Guard, I jumped at the opportunity.

Everyone talked about how hard Basic was, but for me

it flew by. Already used to my dad nagging all the time, being under the close watch of a few drill sergeants felt like no big deal.

When I got back to my hometown in Texas after a few months, they put me in a National Guard unit. Just like Jimmy said, it was a breeze. Once a month, I ironed my uniform, shined my boots and hung around at the unit. We trained on weapons, took long, boring classes and sometimes just sat and did plain nothing. Big-rig trucks sat parked nicely in a row along the back of the motor pool, but we never got to drive them.

Of course, the money I earned really wasn't enough to get by, so I started truck driving part time for a friend. When the harvest seasons rolled around, the jobs came in. I finally found something I enjoyed doing. I could see myself growing up little by little. Keeping busy with work also kept me away from the party scene. I still drank and hung out with my friends, but my busy schedule helped me taper off.

Then the summer after my 19th birthday, I met Leticia. I watched her dancing from across the bar, and I was struck. She was so dang pretty, I just knew I had to meet her. I went up to the dance floor and just started dancing with her. Right away, she smiled. Of course, there wasn't much conversation, but I really had no idea what to say. I was excited to see her a few weeks later at the same club.

The Answer

We ended up sitting at the bar together with drinks in hand, chatting. The music was loud, and my heart raced when she leaned in to hear what I was saying.

"Where are you from?" I shouted.

"Chihuahua, Mexico."

"That's where my parents are from." Right away, we both felt a connection knowing our families were from the same region. We continued to talk and eventually started hanging out. Then one day she rang the bell at my house to meet my parents.

Only a few months later, we were married. Within a few years, Leticia and I had two sons, Junior and Moises, and a large trucking company hired me as an over-the-road driver.

Our life was turning out pretty good together. I felt so much contentment in bringing home a paycheck and supporting my family. On top of that, I actually enjoyed my job. Though I spent long periods away from my family, it really seemed like Leticia understood this sacrifice.

☙☙☙

"What is this, Elisha?" Leticia held up a plastic bag.

"What does it look like, Letty? It's weed."

She stared at me with wide stunned eyes. "Why would you want to do this?" She had never done drugs in her life and possessed a simple, naïve nature. I knew no real way to explain this.

"Babe, this just gets me through the long hours on the road. It's nothing to worry about."

She threw the baggie at me and stalked out of the room.

Along with keeping me from my family, truck driving made my Army drill weekends hard to attend. My bosses didn't really like adjusting to my schedule, and I didn't like the cash I'd miss out on during drill. Finding out that the National Guard system wasn't all that I expected was also discouraging. We didn't do much of anything productive, and after three years with my unit, I had yet to drive a truck. After the Gulf War drawdown, I took advantage of the opportunity and got out. When the discharge papers came in the mail, I was happy with my decision.

In 1994, our daughter Ruth was born. Although our family was growing and my income was good, I felt the pressure of all these responsibilities creeping in like a bad high. Trying to keep Leticia happy, being a father, spending weeks away all became very intense. It made me anxious. When I came home from the road, my muscles ached with fatigue. I wanted to relax and drink a beer, but there was no time for that.

Leticia wanted to go out as a family. The kids wanted to play. With mounting stress at home and little time to rest, the long open road became tiresome. I picked up coke again, and even meth, to get through the extended

The Answer

hours of driving. It seemed to solve the problem. I even had more energy when I got home to my family. But the anxiety remained, and somehow Leticia knew something was just not right.

"You know, Elisha, even when you are home, it's like you're not really here."

"What more do you want? I provide everything for you and the kids. Why can't you just be happy?"

"Because you don't ever talk to me. You never tell me what's really going on inside your head. I have no idea how you feel about me, because you never tell me."

All this emotional talk turned my insides stiff. I wanted to tell her things, but getting them out was just too hard. It was easier to work hard and provide. Wasn't that enough?

"I think this is because of all that drinking you do. Do you realize you are wasting away the best years of our lives?"

I sensed she was right, but I just didn't know how to please her. I sat quietly sipping my beer and watched her storm out of the room.

ঌঌঌ

There has to be more than this, I thought to myself. I wanted to climb to the top. I yearned for status, but this sort of job didn't offer that. However, my friends and co-workers all bought their own trucks and became independent contractors. The idea appealed to me. They decided their hours, their pay, what jobs to take on. What could be better than being my own boss? I'd been driving for five years and felt I was almost an expert in this industry. I knew what it took to make this work.

"This could be good for our family," I told Leticia. Doubt filled her eyes. She continued to fold the laundry without a word.

"I've been driving for a while now; I really think this could work."

"You've only been a truck driver five years, Elisha."

"Exactly, don't you think that's a lot? I've learned so much."

She laid the folded clothes in the laundry basket and got up to leave the room. "You do what you think is best."

I saw this as approval, but really it was surrender. I couldn't see it at the time, but she had no real choice in the matter.

A couple months later, I rolled down the road in my own truck, contracting my own jobs. The money upfront was great — until the expenses piled up. The monthly payment on the truck was $1,500. The insurance was $500, and fuel prices were slowly rising. Maintenance was so expensive that I spent much of my free time trying to do my own tune-up on the massive truck.

Leticia's nagging became relentless. "While you're gone, I answer all the creditor calls. All your time revolves around that stupid truck. I thought you would be home more often."

I returned to the road each week trying to keep from

failing. The stress was more than I could handle, and the drugs weren't cutting it anymore.

Somehow, my mind drifted to my father and the hard work he always did for our family. He tried to warn me about the way I was living, though I never listened. When he changed his life around all those years ago, he turned to God. Maybe I needed to do the same. Instead of music, I started popping in disks of sermons and Bible readings. I convinced Leticia that we needed to go to church, and she agreed. Although the financial struggles didn't go away, I felt better about things. A thought began to whisper to me: *You know the answer to your problems.* As quickly as the thought came, I let the worries and anxieties choke it out. "Just help me out of this mess. Help me get my life back in order, God."

When I returned home, my family no longer ran to the door to see me. My children tiptoed around, trying their best not to anger me. I sat on the couch with the remote in one hand and a beer in the other.

Leticia came into the living room and dropped a stack of papers in my lap. "We are three payments behind on your beloved truck."

I didn't have an answer for her, so I remained silent, watching the television screen.

"Your car was repossessed, Elisha." She waited for a response with her arms crossed and lips pursed in a smirk. The business had been failing since I'd started it two years prior. We'd survived through the last year on credit and now owed more than $90,000.

Dirty Little Secrets

❧❧❧

I called Tom, my old boss, hoping for a way out. "Hey, Tom, how you been? I was wondering if you have any work for me."

"Sure. We can always work something out for you. Where are you looking to go?"

"Well, let me explain. I'm not driving for myself anymore. That just got a little too out of hand for my family and me. I'm actually looking for a job."

Tom remained silent for a moment. I hoped he was stunned and not disappointed. "Sure, Elisha. You always were a hard worker. Come in next week, and we'll get you started again."

I hung up the phone and immediately sensed so much weight lift from my chest. I felt like I could suddenly breathe after only one phone call. Was this an answered prayer? I wasn't convinced just yet, but God did have my attention.

Without the stress of my own business, life slowed down a little. I was still on the road nearly every week, but Leticia certainly was relieved. I did what I could to satisfy her, and things seemed to go better.

Our family continued to attend church on a regular basis, and sometimes we even saw family members at the service. My cousin Nick went to the same church. He had joined the Army eight years before and seemed to be doing well.

"Yeah, it's a pretty good job. It's stressful at times, but

it's all worth it in the end," he said as we met in the church lobby.

"What do they have you doing?"

"I'm a recruiter," he said with a chuckle. "But, you know, my family is taken care of with insurance and healthcare. I'll get a retirement if I stay in the full 20. This is pretty much what I needed."

"What would it take to get me back in the Army?"

"It really wouldn't take much. Just bring your discharge papers to my office, and I can take a look and let you know."

This conversation started me thinking about a whole new direction. The National Guard was a real joke, but this would be the full-time Army. I could get back the camaraderie, the structured lifestyle, a sense of purpose. I could really take pride in the work I did.

"Maybe this is what our family needs."

"I've heard this before. You said the same thing about your business that put us in bankruptcy."

"This is different. I can get us healthcare, insurance, a retirement."

"If this is what you want to do, then go ahead and do it."

A few months later, I was in job training, and I missed the birth of our fourth child, Araceli. I graduated a few weeks later, and our family was relocated to Hawaii in the spring of 2001.

I jumped straight into an Infantry unit with

enthusiasm. My work ethic earned the respect of my bosses and peers right away. My charm and personality gained me friends in my unit from the get-go. However, my church attendance dwindled, and my alcoholism resurfaced. All this attention went straight to my head, and Leticia suffered through my arrogant attitude.

One night I arrived home well after midnight to find her waiting. Anger flashed in her eyes. I got into bed and rolled over.

"When is this going to stop? You said this Army thing would be good for our family."

"You know what, Leticia? I call the shots around here. I provide everything you and the kids need. You have no right to complain about anything."

"What is this, Elisha? Because this sure isn't a marriage. I'm tired of all your drinking and yelling."

"All you ever do is complain. When are you going to learn to keep your mouth shut?" Even in the dim light of the bedside lamp, I saw in her eyes the pain I caused, but I wasn't sure if I cared anymore. I loved her so much, but I was tired of her nagging. I didn't know what she wanted. This emotional, touchy-feely thing wasn't for me.

Our conversation hung heavy on my mind through the next day at work. I drove straight home that afternoon instead of hanging out with the guys. I walked into the living room where my kids were laughing and watching television. They caught one glimpse of me and quickly fell silent. Ruth and Moises ran down the hall to their room. I didn't realize my attitude affected more than just Leticia. I

The Answer

found her in the kitchen feeding Araceli a bottle. She looked up with a scowl and turned her back.

"I'm sorry about last night." She responded with silence. "Listen, I thought we could try counseling. I want to change …"

She erupted into laughter and looked at me, bewildered. "I've been dealing with this for 10 years, Elisha. All you ever talk about is changing and what is good for our family, but, really, you have no clue." She walked out of the room, leaving me sitting at the table alone. My wife had given up on me, my children were afraid of me and I couldn't admit that it was my own fault.

Leticia pretty much shut down at this point. She stopped talking to me and started living like I wasn't even there. She and the kids went out, met friends and did things in Hawaii like I didn't exist.

My unit prepared to leave for Iraq in 2006. We were replacing the 101st Airborne Division. These guys had seen a rough deployment and had lost several men. All of us expected hard times ahead, but we didn't realize just how bad it would be.

The reality of our situation quickly set in. Within the first three months in Iraq, we lost two soldiers and one civilian contractor. I felt like my faith was a yo-yo spinning back and forth, but I knew deep down that voice was right, God was the answer. When I woke in the morning to the dusty light shining in the tent flap, I prayed, *God, forgive me. Forgive all my sins, and protect me in this day.* I knew enough from church to know I needed to be forgiven. I knew I had done so much wrong, especially to my family and marriage.

After only three months in Iraq, I was sent home for vacation time. Hunter and I flew together. We both agreed that it seemed early in the deployment to even think about going home.

"Well, at least we get to see our family," I said to him.

"Yeah, that's the truth. I'm going to see my 2-month-old baby," he said, pulling down his bag from the overhead compartment. We walked off the plane into Dallas Airport. "My gate's this way."

"All right, man, enjoy your family while it lasts." I walked the opposite way and never saw him again.

It took two extra days to get all the way home to Hawaii. I was happy to see my family and grateful for my children, but a deep feeling of discontent hung heavy in our home. My kids played their video games in the same room but didn't seem to notice me. My wife went about her routine like any other day. On top of it all, the uneasiness wouldn't let me relax. The thought of my soldiers on patrol each day while I kicked back on my couch bothered me. I had grown close to many of the guys in my unit, and they now felt like my only real friends.

"What's wrong with you?" Leticia asked with a groggy voice. She was half asleep, but I lay on my back, eyes wide open. I didn't feel like telling her what I was thinking.

"I got jetlag. My system's all out of whack."

We celebrated Thanksgiving with our kids and some friends. Before I knew it, my time arrived to head back to

The Answer

Iraq. We said goodbye at the airport like I was leaving for any other trip. Leticia's heart seemed just as cold as mine. At the time, I just couldn't see I had caused all this myself.

"We're glad to have you back," my platoon sergeant said, shaking my hand. "It's been rough out here, so it's good to have you back in the game. We want you to get reacclimatized and situated, so you'll be sitting out this week. You can sit in the command center and watch and get familiar with the way we are doing things right now. You'll get back on the patrols next week."

The next morning, I entered the command center and reviewed the list of soldiers going on patrol that day. Hunter topped the list. He had just returned from leave like me and was already back in the trucks.

"What's going on with Hunter?" I asked my commander. "Didn't he just get back, too?"

"He did, two days ago. But he's got some new soldiers in his squad. They're young ones so he wants to make sure they know what they're doing."

I napped in my tent later that day when another soldier burst in. "An IED hit! One of our patrols is in bad shape."

We both ran out of the tent to the command center. Listening to the busy radio traffic brought grim news. I sat on a bench, hearing the emergency response teams calling for body bags. In my head, I ran through a list of who had gone out that day. I knew Hunter was out there. Our lieutenant came in and sat down at the table in the center of the room. He pulled off his hat and rubbed his forehead.

"They're all dead," he said, staring down into his lap.

Five soldiers died that day. Hunter rode in the truck that got hit, along with another new father, Simpson. But Simpson never even got to meet his son.

A helicopter landed, and we scrambled through our Humvees, searching for extra body bags. When the helicopter returned, the remains of our comrades arrived in the black bags.

My insides grew hollow that day, as if something inside me went dark. I didn't know it at the time, but it was my emotions. I decided I wasn't going to feel anything. It was the only way I could function without losing it.

While it got me through the days, it sure made things hard for my soldiers and everyone around me. Instead of leading by example and encouraging my troops, I yelled orders. I made unreasonable demands. My standards were high, and these guys were only 19 and 20 years old. They were young and inexperienced, and my temper ran hot. I thought I was toughening them up, but, really, they were pulsating with fear on the inside.

Going outside the gates was tough for all of us. The silent question rang in everyone's mind: *Will I come back through this gate later today?* While the fear made most guys vigilant, it made me ruthless. But I still prayed, "God, I don't know if this is my day. Please forgive my sins." Deep down, I knew this hollow anger was wrong.

The Answer

We patrolled the city one scorching afternoon. Hot beads of sweat ran along my brow. A group of suspicious-looking kids eyed us from the corner. We were always on the lookout for odd behavior. "What do you think of that group over there?" I asked Scott.

"I don't know, man. They just look like thugs to me, nothing serious. We can go question them if you want."

"I just got a funny feeling about them."

We walked over and started asking them for names and what they were doing. The oldest kid held his chin high and spoke in Arabic. His dark brown eyes scowled. I grabbed his shirt and pushed him against the wall. "Listen here, kid. Pay attention."

Scott pulled me off the boy and got up in my face. "You gotta calm down. These aren't the guys we're looking for."

I didn't care what Scott or anyone thought. I felt the right and the power to treat these people this way. After watching body bags with our comrades' remains coming and going, these guys were just another threat.

The next day, we swept through the village, collecting all the men 16 and older, taking them to the mosque. A team scanned fingerprints and irises. They were creating a digital database to keep track and possibly catch men engaging in terrorist activity. Most of the men in the village obeyed our orders.

We knocked at the door to the home of an old man and his son. "You all need to get to the mosque, now!" I yelled. It was obvious this old man didn't understand our

English. He hobbled out of his house speaking in Arabic. I grabbed him by the arm and yelled, while pointing at the mosque. "You go there, now."

"Put him in the truck; the man can't walk," Scott said.

"No. This man will walk," I said, pushing him in the direction of the mosque.

"Listen, you're getting out of hand," Scott whispered between clenched teeth.

I looked at the man and his son standing helpless on the road. We put them on the hood of the Humvee and drove them to the mosque.

About a month later, our commander decided to build an outpost near the location of the recent IED hit. With so much activity in that area, our presence there was supposed to discourage terrorists from placing IEDs. My platoon was sent out to the site.

Davis and I pulled a guard shift inside the concrete barriers on a hot afternoon. We stood in full gear, making small talk about our plans back home. The sun's rays beat down and reflected off the sand. I wiped my brow with a cloth from my pocket and looked around. In the next moment, a bright light flashed, and Davis collapsed to the floor, hands gripping his head. The earth shook, and a large boom caused my ears to ring with a loud pitched buzzing. A cloud of smoke and dust obscured my vision as I tried to squint through the haze. Davis lifted his head. "What the h*** was that?"

I didn't realize that I, too, had crouched down to the

The Answer

floor. "I don't know, but we're alive." Soldiers poured out of tents, surprised to see us lying in the dirt.

We went to the command post to report what happened. We weren't even sure what happened, but we let our leadership know we were alive.

"Take four of your men, and patrol the site. A truck loaded with explosives attempted to breach the wall where you and Davis were located." The hollow space inside me grew as I went to round up my squad. I picked my most experienced men, and we loaded up our Humvee.

"Protect us God," I prayed as we exited the gate. Flames still engulfed the truck, and the smell of burning rubber and oil hung heavy with the black clouds of smoke. Pieces of engine and metal lay scattered everywhere. It was like walking through a dream. A car sat parked behind the dump truck, and my heart raced. This could very well be another car bomb. We pointed our loaded weapons and approached the vehicle. To our surprise, the man driving the car had also survived the blast. We made him exit the vehicle. Blood covered his face, torso and arms. We got the man medical care and continued to survey the area.

Pieces of the suicide bomber lay scattered hundreds of meters away from the dump truck. We looked down at the man's mangled torso. The stench of death was overwhelming, and still, I only felt hollow looking down at the body. His face was still connected to his body, but the skull, bones and eyes were all disintegrated. His face looked like an empty mask — as empty as I felt.

The explosives investigation team showed up and

collected evidence. They concluded the dump truck was intended to breach our walls, and a series of suicide car bombers were supposed to enter through the hole.

An investigator pointed out a large crater in the ground. "You all are lucky to be alive. The magnitude of this explosion is unreal. You really should be dead."

This was not luck, this was the hand of God. There was no doubt in my mind that God had protected us that day. Still, my relentless hollow feeling didn't change. We had stood so close to death, I really wondered, *What else can possibly happen?*

The sun made the day nearly unbearable as we waited on watch keeping a perimeter in our Humvees. Our trucks surrounded a possible bomb found by the explosives team in the nearby village. The tension thickened as each soldier watched his area for incoming rounds or suspicious activity.

The attacks didn't cease, even when our replacement brigade showed up. We were relieved, but our fatalities climbed to 16. We lost one last soldier only two weeks before coming home at the end of our deployment.

༄༄༄

Returning home, getting away from the death toll and being free from the war brought relief. But coming back brought its own battles. My hollow state and lack of emotions that helped me get through each day didn't

The Answer

automatically shut off. The images of what we went through didn't just get wiped away. Every soldier went through a long series of meetings, questionnaires and interviews, but I managed to manipulate my answers. Army psychologists concluded I was fit for work.

Being with my family caused more struggle. The issues we faced before this 14-month deployment slowly began to resurface. Before I left, I was already failing at my role as a husband and father, and I couldn't even see it. Now I added the struggle of dealing with thoughts, images and guilt of everything that happened over the past year. On top of all of that, Leticia was clueless about this turmoil. She only saw the same calloused alcoholic she had always known.

"Do you know what your daughter told me, Elisha? She said, 'When Dad comes home, my life will be over.' I know you went through a lot, but we are not soldiers. We are your family, and you have to start treating us better."

I had no words for her. Her face all twisted in anguish bothered me, but my cold demeanor said otherwise. "Why don't we try family counseling?"

"I already told you that I don't want to do that. All I know is you need to change. If you don't change, I don't want to be by your side."

☙☙☙

Only a few months after the deployment, we relocated to Fort Polk, Louisiana. We were going to be in an airborne unit, something I had always wanted to do in my career. I told myself a geographic change was just what I needed. Being in a new place would help resolve my inner conflicts, leaving the past behind.

But I was wrong. My thoughts didn't change. The cold attitude on life and actions toward my family remained the same. I wanted desperately to be a good father and husband, but I just couldn't. Leticia and I seriously considered a divorce. Things only got worse with all the relocations the Army sent me through. We moved to Fort Bragg, North Carolina, then the Army wanted to send me to Fort Drum. Leticia put her foot down. Tired of moving, she wanted stability for our family. I talked to my branch manager and got sent to Korea for a year, thinking this was a better option. The kids could stay in their own schools, Junior would graduate and not have to move his senior year and Leticia would be happy. We reconciled and decided to stay together.

But being away and alone gave me the freedom to drink my worries away. I used up every bit of our savings. Leticia had enough. She stopped accepting my calls and didn't return my messages.

Despite our differences, she bought a home in Fort Bragg using my VA loan. Thinking to appease her, I signed all the necessary paperwork and let her pick the house. It didn't matter to me. All I wanted was peace. It only got worse when the Army cut me orders to become a drill sergeant for two years in Fort Benning, Georgia. It was a seven-hour drive to visit my family.

The Answer

I walked in the front door and received my usual welcome, a wave from the couch from my kids and a glance from my wife in the kitchen. I sat down with my two sons. They focused on the television with all their concentration on a racing game. I went to the kitchen to find my wife cooking Mexican food. She looked up from the stove and said, "How was your week?"

I hugged her and kissed her on the cheek as she turned away from my lips. I knew better than to expect more than this. I felt like a roommate in my own home.

I was offered a job at Fort Jackson, South Carolina, as an instructor at the drill sergeant school. This was only two hours away from my family, so I accepted right away. With a closer commute and less demanding job, I could come home every weekend. Leticia began to drop her guard. She warmed up, perhaps because she saw me trying.

I came home to my family and began to feel more welcomed. I really thought things were looking up.

"I want a new car, babe," Leticia told me one night as we got ready for bed.

"A new car? What for?"

"Well, the kids are older, we don't need car seats anymore and I have had that SUV forever now."

"Have you already started looking?"

She glanced over from across the room while combing her hair. "I've always wanted a Corvette," she said, smiling. I thought this would make her happy and told her to go for it.

Dirty Little Secrets

Before long, our relationship slowly returned to its calloused state after her big purchase. Back to ignored calls and cold welcomes. It seemed she refused to work things out with me.

"You have put me through so much. I don't even know what to do anymore, Elisha."

"We need to stop this bouncing back and forth. I'm tired of making an effort and then being ignored. We need to just file for divorce and leave it at that."

"I'm not ready to divorce. When the kids are grown, and I don't need you anymore, then I will divorce you." She looked me straight in the eyes and tightened her jaw. I was still so hollow and empty that her words hardly brought pain. I felt more insulted than anything else. I got up and left early to return to Fort Jackson for the weekend.

I took vacation time from work and went home to Texas with my son Moises. It felt good to see my family, and of course, I ended up reconnecting with friends. We hung out at a club in nearby El Paso and drank one beer after another.

I drove home well below the speed limit, struggling through blurred vision, when I saw the flashing red and blue lights behind me. My heart sank as I sat handcuffed in the back of a cop car. I was too ashamed to call my parents, so I bailed myself out. I called my sister for a ride in the morning.

"Are you serious, Elisha?"

"Yeah, just come pick me up. I already bailed myself

The Answer

out. I haven't told Mom and Dad anything, and I really don't plan on it."

She arrived an hour later with my son in the backseat. Seeing the disappointment all over my son's face made me feel like a failure. My phone buzzed with messages as I turned it back on.

The first one came from my commanding officer. "El Paso police called us and let us know the situation. Call us as soon as you get bailed out."

I knew from that moment I was going to lose my career. I flew back to Fort Bragg and dropped my son off. I couldn't face my wife and didn't even bother. I had no choice but to return to my leadership to face the humiliation.

I sat in my commander's office as he flipped through a stack of papers. He looked up at me with a stoic face. "You are suspended from all duties until your investigation is over." He watched me, waiting for an answer. I had no words. "Do you know what this means for your career?"

"Yes, sir. I am aware of my consequences." I knew it was only a matter of time before I was separated from the Army. It only got worse when the post commander reprimanded me.

That night, I called my wife to let her know what happened. I planned to tell her everything.

"You know I came back early from my vacation."

"Yeah, your job just needed you back so badly, right?"

"No, Letty. I got a DUI in El Paso. I am suspended here at work."

"Oh," she said and paused. "Well, all right, I guess." Her nonchalant attitude made my anger burn hot. She couldn't care less about what was going on. A few weeks later, she asked for a divorce, and this time there was no looking back. After 21 years of marriage, she had finally had enough.

❧❧❧

I started living one day at a time. Each day I sat at work in my office with little to do. I still earned a paycheck during my investigation, so I was obligated to show up. It was like I had set my whole life on fire. Everything I worked so hard for was turning to ash. My family hated me. My career was ending in humiliation. I had few friends left now that I was in trouble. However, Baker, another soldier in our unit, started showing up in my office. Instead of judging me, he encouraged me.

"You need to get back to praying," he said. He always brought God to the forefront of my mind. "You know what? You already know the answer. Christ is the answer to your problems."

His words struck deep. It was funny to hear the same words I had always felt down deep coming from him.

"Why don't you come to church with me this weekend?"

I searched my mind for an excuse. But, really, I had none. "Yeah, you know what? I think I will."

From the first day I attended Vive Church, I felt

welcomed. Little by little, Pastor Randy's words cut more cracks in my calloused attitude. God used him to reach me.

My insides spun with dread as the line rang. I was finally calling my dad to let him know what happened.

"Hello, son. How have you been?"

"To be honest, not too good, Dad. There are things I have to tell you." I paused, and he waited for me to go on. "When I visited you during vacation … I got a DUI. I'm suspended from work right now, and I might lose my job."

He let out a heavy sigh, and I braced myself for a long "I told you so" lecture. "That's a heavy load to be carrying, son. I hope you realize you can't do it alone." His response stunned me. "You're going to need a lot of support to get through this. I hope you are going back to church. Christ is the answer to getting you through this."

I could actually feel God talking through my dad, just like in church. "I've been going to church with a co-worker, actually."

"I'm glad to hear it. Your mother and I are here for you, and we will be praying for you. At some point, you're going to have to stop running from God. Praying and going to church is good, but you need to surrender your life and accept what he has for you."

I knew he was right. I carried his words with me in the back of my mind. Things didn't get much easier at work. In order for me to keep my job, I had to join a 12-step program and go to outpatient recovery therapy. I resented the fact that the Army was pushing me into this, but, really, this was all part of God's plan. I had to talk to counselors and therapists almost daily. In the 12-step program, I began admitting that I had a problem and I needed help.

I drove home one evening after a therapy session and realized that I had just spent an hour talking about my emotions, and it wasn't that bad. I began working through all the stuff pent up inside. I arrived at my barracks and sat on the edge of my bed thinking about the past few months. I placed my head in my hands, bowed my head and prayed. *God, I'm so tired. My life is pretty much broken, and I have no way of fixing it. I want to just give it over to you. I really need forgiveness, and more than that, I need you in my life. Just take this broken life, God, and have your way with it.*

It was a simple prayer, and I didn't see any bright light or feel any overwhelming emotions. Somehow, I believed that God was really going to work in my life. Through the 14 months of nearly dying and witnessing death in Iraq, I had offered shallow prayers to God but refused to really give myself over to him. But this was it. I was at the very bottom of my pit, and I believed God wanted to lift me out.

I woke up the next morning with a sense of peace. My family and career were still in disorder, but I felt confident it was going to be okay.

Pastor Randy started counseling me one-on-one, and my recovery jumped to the next level. I felt a subtle peace taking over my life. My anger started to melt away, and I saw myself becoming a new person.

I returned to El Paso in early 2013 to attend court and answer for my DUI. My attorney left me feeling little comfort about the situation. I decided to accept the consequences and let God help me through. I waited while my attorney spoke to the judge. He came out of the judge's quarters with a smile and slapped me on the back.

"Things are looking up for you, Elisha. You're going to be enrolled in the Pre-Trial Diversion Program. This is a program in the State of Texas for first-time offenders. You will have one year of probation, pay fines and, since you have no priors, your case will be dismissed at the end of your time."

Again, I was certain God's hand had swept through my life, taking care of me. I knew I deserved whatever the court gave me, but God handed me a portion of his kindness.

☞☞☞

"Why do you constantly call me, Elisha? Don't you take hints?"

"I want to see you and the kids, Leticia."

"What for? You know how they feel about you. Do you really want to put yourself through that?"

I was sure Leticia complained to the kids about me. I figured she had told them every bad thing she possibly could about me.

But God was putting my life back together, and I knew he would help me in this as well.

"Just give me one day with them. You already know I haven't been drinking." Even though it was too late for us, I focused on speaking with kindness and patience.

"That's nothing but a lie. You are never going to quit." The truth was, I had been sober for several months. "You can have them on Saturday, but I really don't want to see you."

I picked up the kids that weekend and took them to a park. They wanted to play at the basketball court, but we sat at a picnic table instead.

"I really want to talk to you guys all together. I know you have been through a lot because of me and my alcoholism. I am not going to make you any promises about the future, but I do want you to know that my actions are going to speak louder than my words."

I could say these words with confidence now because I had Christ within me getting me through the hard stuff. All those years, I had done things my way. Now it was time to let God take the lead.

Reporting to a probation officer was a humbling experience. But being part of Vive Church and attending a Bible study for military veterans taught me the value of humility, among many other things. I learned that God used every situation to mold me into what he wanted me to be. Eight months into my probation, my attorney called and said I was done with the Diversion Program. I received a packet in the mail dismissing all charges.

The Answer

My kids have seen my words come to life, and they see God working in me. Junior has even expressed a willingness to spend time with me, just the two of us, having a burger, spending the weekend together. It reminds me of being a kid and watching my own father overcome alcoholism through the power of Christ. It's funny, because even my commander has taken note of the change in my life. I have sat several times in her office and had conversations about Vive Church and my recovery.

For a while, I constantly prayed for God to fix everything. Now, I realize that God has already done so much for me. I have started praying for God to use my life as an example to others. The thing is, this reconciliation with my kids, getting a fresh start in my career, my DUI being wiped from my record — none of it was my doing. The answers to all the problems I created in my life came only after seeking and accepting the forgiveness and healing power of Christ.

Conclusion

My heart is full. When I became a pastor, my desire was to change the world. My hope was to see people encouraged and those who were hurting filled with hope. As I read this book, I saw that passion being fulfilled. However, at Vive Church, rather than being content with our past victories, we are spurred on to believe that many more can occur.

Every time we see another life change, it increases our awareness that God really loves people, and he is actively seeking to change lives. Think about it: How did you get this book? We believe you read this book because God brought it to you, seeking to reveal his love to you. Whether you're a man or a woman, a teacher or a waitress, blue collar or no collar, a parent or a student, military or civilian, we believe God came to save you. He came to save us. He came to save them. He came to save all of us from the hellish pain in which we've wallowed and to offer real joy and the opportunity to share in real life that will last forever through faith in Jesus Christ.

Do you have honest questions that such real change is possible? It seems too good to be true, doesn't it? We at Vive Church invite you to be our guest and meet our church family. Freely ask questions, find your place to belong and see if we're "for real." Journey with us at whatever pace you are comfortable. You will find that we are far from perfect. Our scars and sometimes open wounds are still healing, but we just want you to know God is still completing the process of bringing us to life. We still make mistakes in our journey, like everyone will. Therefore, we acknowledge our continued need for each other's forgiveness and support. We need the love of God just as much as we did the day before we believed in him.

If you are unable to be with us, yet you intuitively sense you would really like to experience such a life change, here are some basic thoughts to consider. If you choose, at the end of this conclusion, you can pray the suggested prayer. If your prayer genuinely comes from your heart, you will experience the beginning stages of authentic life change, similar to those you have read about.

How does this change occur?

Recognize that what you're doing isn't working. Accept the fact that Jesus desires to forgive you for your bad decisions and selfish motives. Realize that without this forgiveness, you will continue a life separated from God and his amazing love. In the Bible, the book of Romans, chapter 6, verse 23 tells us that the result of sin (seeking our way rather than God's way) is death, but the gift that God freely gives is everlasting life found in Jesus Christ.

Believe in your heart that God passionately loves you and wants to give you a new heart. Ezekiel 11:19 reads, "I will give them singleness of heart and put a new spirit within them. I will take away their stony, stubborn heart and give them a tender, responsive heart" (NLT).

Conclusion

Believe in your heart that "If you confess with your mouth that Jesus is Lord and believe in your heart that God raised him from the dead, you will be saved" (Romans 10:9 NLT).

Believe in your heart that because Jesus paid for your failure and wrong motives, and because you asked him to forgive you, he has filled your new heart with his life in such a way that he transforms you from the inside out. Second Corinthians 5:17 (Living Bible) reads, "When someone becomes a Christian, he becomes a brand new person inside. He is not the same anymore. A new life has begun!"

Why not pray now?

Lord Jesus, if I've learned one thing in my journey, it's that you are God and I am not. My choices have not resulted in the happiness I hoped they would bring. Not only have I experienced pain, I've also caused it. I know I am separated from you, but I want that to change. I am sorry for the choices I've made that have hurt myself, others and denied you. I believe your death paid for my sins, and you are now alive to change me from the inside out. Would you please do that now? I ask you to come and live in me so that I can sense you are here with me. Thank you for hearing and changing me. Now please help me know when you are talking to me, so I can cooperate with your efforts to change me. Amen.

Dirty Little Secrets

The Midlands' unfolding story of God's love is still being written ... and your name is in it.

I hope to see you this Sunday!

Randy Knechtel
Vive Church
Columbia, South Carolina

We would love for you to join us at Vive Church!

We meet Sunday mornings at 9:30 and 11:15 a.m. at 2630 Clemson Road, Columbia, SC 29229.

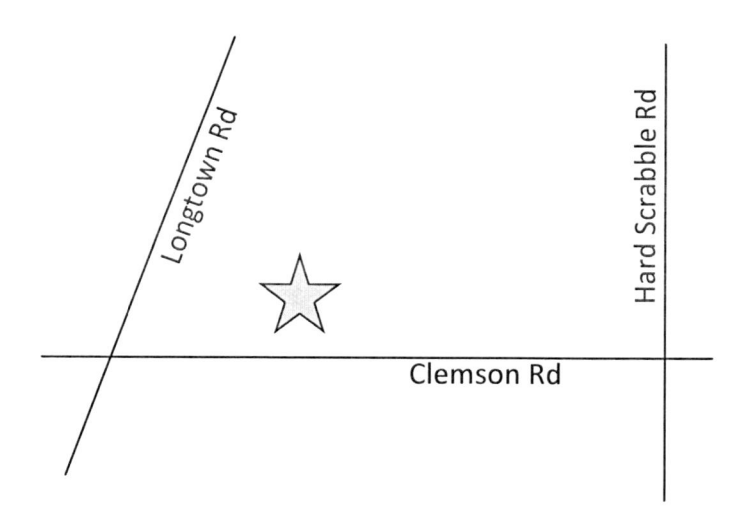

You can contact us in any of the following ways:
Phone: 803.233.2877
Web site: www.vivechurch.com
Facebook: www.facebook.com/vivecolumbia
Twitter: www.twitter.com/vivechurch
E-mail: info@vivechurch.com

Watch live or On-Demand at:
www.vivechurch.com/watch-live

For more information on reaching your city with stories from your church, go to www.testimonybooks.com.

Good Catch Publishing

Did one of these stories touch you?
Did one of these real people move you to tears?
Tell us (and them) about it on our Facebook page at www.facebook.com/GoodCatchPublishing.